Social Media Judo

Chris Aarons, Geoff Nelson and Nick White
with
Dan Zehr

First published by Dog Ear Publishing
4010 W. 86th Street, Ste H
Indianapolis, IN 46268
www.dogearpublishing.net

ISBN: 978-160844-885-2

This book is printed on acid-free paper.

Printed in the United States of America

Dedication

Thanks to everyone who helped with this book: Tom Augenthaler, Halley Bass and Terri Stratton as well as Wendi Aarons and Carrie Nelson, who are all invaluable to our company. And a special thanks to Sally Nelson, who helped with the endless proofing and sanity checks.

Also, a very special thank you to all the bloggers whose passion brings us information we want and many times the things we never knew existed.

To Mom,
Thanks for everything
I am today

Love Garth

Foreword

IN SPITE OF INITIAL EN masse cluelessness, companies are finally beginning to understand the necessity of social media in relation to their businesses. Because the term "social media" itself is so ambiguous, it should come as no surprise that the old-guard number runners and boardroom potentates at the top (and out of touch) took so long to get it. To my fellow content producers and me, this idea never took getting used to—because it's something we've known and used all along: progress is limitless with true two-way communications that utilize readily accessible (and relatively universal) tools. Sure, because of its more "organic" nature, this social-media thing is more difficult for a company to control than traditional marketing programs. It's refreshing to see more and more denizens of the corporate world waking up to the value of something that, by its very nature, can't be fully supervised. From the perspective of upper management, it's got to be a scary adjustment.

No doubt, progress has come in fits and starts. After decades—even centuries—of one-way messaging, entities have grown all too accustomed to the command-and-conquer mindset. Today, though, they're starting to come face-to-face with this new realization: They can't really control what's happening on the Internet. They can exert an influence (hopefully, a positive one), but the one-way streets are in the rearview mirror (lined on both sides, I imagine, with a crowd of giant football-style foam hands waving goodbye).

Fortunately for all the content producers and influencers of the social-media ecosystem, companies that learn to grow past this controlling mindset become, like an old Jedi master I once knew, "more powerful than you can possibly imagine." Unfortunately, far too many businesses have yet to reach this point, so let me add my own little bit of advice as a preamble for the guys at Ivy Worldwide: As a business leader, you have to quit dipping your toe in the water for testing and simply get a strategy and jump in. As I write this in the middle of summer, I confess that the concept sounds more refreshing than terrifying. Dive in! Enjoy!

Sure, it takes time to learn how to swim, and it takes years to learn to swim at the highest levels. It'll take practice to get really good at generating word-of-mouth marketing campaigns, but with a solid strategy, jumping in and trying is far less dangerous than avoiding the jump indefinitely. You can make mistakes in this world and still retain brand loyalty and support—in most cases. To paraphrase Bobby Scott and Bob Russell, "It ain't heavy—it's social media."

The only perceived weight of social media comes from that legacy of corporate control. For the whole stretch of history until now, businesses could take a new medium and mold it into their marketing processes. Now, like the Chicago River more than a century ago, the dynamic has been reversed to flow in the opposite direction. Behind every online review, blog post, or screen name is a real person—a real consumer who's responding to and sharing his or her impression of your product or message, or his or her perception of your company as a whole. A business that "gets" social media will embrace this for the opportunities that it offers instead of shying away from it entirely (think of the ostrich with its head in the sand) or trying to stifle its influence with laughably obsolete corporate strong-arm tactics.

Online conversations and relationships may be fairly new games in town, but the consequences of these interactions have the ability to transcend their old-school "real-world" (whatever that means these days) equivalents. Never before have so many been so empowered with voices that mean so much to so many. An everyday person's online entity doesn't rely on a publishing contract, a television show, a radio broadcast, or a luckily landed letter to the editor to express an opinion. With the advent and increasing use of the Internet and the many ways it allows our species to interact, Andy Warhol's predicted 15 minutes of fame for all has become so much more. If you want it, you've got your own modern-day, globally spanning version of the book, the television show, the radio broadcast, the newspaper—really, a soapbox of any dimension you can imagine—to let your words be read or seen or heard. The impact you make in the overall social-media spectrum is up to you and your perseverance, but the tools are there for anyone with an Internet connection. Again, a business that remains dormant to these facts and clings strictly to yesterday's ways will find itself more out of touch than a porcupine applying for work in a balloon factory. To someone who is completely new to true community communications, figuring out how to use social media, and use it well, can be daunting and seemingly impossible to figure out, but it CAN be done.

I first met Chris Aarons, Geoff Nelson, and Nick White in their previous lives. Chris and Geoff worked for Advanced Micro Devices (AMD) while Nick was with Microsoft. Unfortunately for Nick, this was also during a period of time when Windows Vista—an operating system that I found extremely difficult to recommend to anybody—shipped. In fact, I was quite vocal about my discontent with the direction of the platform at the time, and I was somewhat lambasted by the greater Microsoft Windows community. Long story short: years later, my assertions were widely accepted—and my integrity remained wholly intact.

Very few traditional PR and marketing professionals know how to deal with that level of criticism. They'll sweep it under the rug or try to poke at it from every angle but the direct one. Nick was as direct as he could be and always took the time to really listen to what I had to say. If he felt as though he didn't understand where I was coming from with something, he would take the time to ask.

Back then, Chris didn't work for Microsoft, but his job at AMD made him an intermediary of sorts for the software giant. Working at one of Microsoft's industry partners put him in a very different position than Nick's. Chris had to play a co-marketing game, so to speak. He understood that countless "geeks" couldn't throw full support behind something that we didn't feel warranted that support. He also knew that, had I tried to support it, my audience would have taken me to the mat immediately. Chris understood this quite well. If a product isn't quite up to snuff, it isn't anybody's fault but the company's. If you want positive buzz, why create something unworthy of receiving it?

Nick, Chris, and Geoff jumped into the pool a while back, learning how to stay afloat in the deep end. Today, I would consider them to be world-class swimmers and coaches in the pool. With any luck, the stragglers will join them soon.

Oh, and please don't get hung up on the term "social media"—next year, the marketers will be calling it something else.

Chris Pirillo
chris@pirillo.com
@ChrisPirillo (on Twitter)

Introduction

AT IVY WORLDWIDE, WE'VE ORCHESTRATED some of the most successful word-of-mouth marketing programs in the last few years, but we had to survive one of the worst car wrecks of a campaign to get there.

The final weeks of 2006 were slipping away, and the pending release of Microsoft's Windows Vista operating system loomed on the horizon. The launch felt especially critical for the software titan. Its long-held dominance over the home-computing environment faced challenges from both Apple and Linux as well as Google and a host of other Web-based applications that threatened to dilute the demand for software on the PC. After watching new rivals take fuller advantage of the Internet's potential to change the market, Microsoft was not about to sit idly by as social media grew more and more popular. The marketing machine for Vista would include a major social-media push. The company asked Nick White to help run it.

Around the same time, Advanced Micro Devices (AMD) had gone on a roll. The company's Opteron microprocessor had carved away some of Intel's dominance in the server and workstation markets. Its processors for home computers took a ride on the wave of popularity, too. AMD had no hope of seriously challenging Intel's market-share advantage, but Chris Aarons and Geoff Nelson managed to work up a rising online buzz for the underdog company's products.

When Microsoft started rounding up partners to join the marketing push for Vista, then, it wasn't long before the three of us – Nick, Chris and Geoff – would meet. We and our partners on the larger social-media campaign decided to work with some of the most notable bloggers and online content producers, the people whose thumbs-up or thumbs-down on Vista would influence millions of potential customers. The goal was clear: Build some positive buzz for Vista, perhaps even take the edge off the skepticism that was rising about the software in the greater computing community, and perhaps generate some sales for AMD in the process.

In retrospect, the plan sounds like a no-brainer. But when the three of us started working on the Vista launch, no one had come up with any real set of instructions for online word-of-mouth marketing. Popular pundits such as Robert Scoble, Andy Sernovitz, and others had detailed a 30,000-foot view of how to play online—be transparent, engage in conversations, have an authentic voice—but no one had a true understanding of the nuts and bolts of a successful online marketing program from the company side. And, more to the point, no one knew how to go about driving demand generation for a product or brand and positively impact the business metrics that ultimately matter (and that we as professional marketers are paid to influence). It was the Wild West of the online word-of-mouth marketing era: Shoot from the hip and hope you hit the target.

So, the three of us took our shot. We figured we could generate some buzz for the Vista launch by putting the software in the hands of 128 influential online content producers. We would load Vista on top-of-the-line PCs, including Acer's high-end Ferrari notebooks, then send the PCs out to the influencers and let the chips fall where they may. If all went well, as we and our colleagues hoped, three things would happen:

1. Microsoft would tap into and grow the momentum generated by its outside evangelists.
2. Our efforts would generate positive word of mouth for Vista and AMD.
3. Some of the naysayers would appreciate the hands-on experience of Vista enough to actually reverse trend and recommend the product.

In theory, it was a good approach—and then the letters went out.

Edelman, Microsoft's outside PR firm, sent letters to 120 of the selected influencers, telling them that shiny new AMD computers loaded with Windows Vista Ultimate would soon arrive at their doorsteps. "No strings attached," the letter basically said. "Do with it what you will—and by all means, feel free to blog about it."The letter did not ask them if they cared to receive anything in the first place. It didn't ask them to send the laptop back or give it away. In fact, it didn't say much at all. The vague message spawned a wave of confusion among its recipients. Was this a gift? Was it a bribe? Was it fodder for a giveaway? Or was it simply a review unit to evaluate, blog about, and send back to the company? No one really knew.

While the letters were the source of some confusion, an explosion of outright vitriol occurred after eight bloggers were sent Acer Ferrari notebooks without first receiving any sort of heads-up. One of these eight people was Australian blogger Long Zheng, who runs Istartedsomething.com, which had a relatively small but devoted following at the time. He wasn't the first to post a note or review about the nice new computer that Microsoft, Acer, and AMD had sent him—but his post was one of the first to ask an ethical question about what he called the Christmas presents: "It retails for a hot $2,299. But if you write about Microsoft, they might even give you one for free," he wrote. "Is it ethical? Probably not. Is it worth something to hard-working sweat and tears bloggers? Hell yeah."

Who knows if the Edelman letter would've clarified things for Zheng, but having received no warning about the PCs at all surely didn't help. Nor did Scoble's post soon afterward, in which he made no bones at all about his take on the program: "Scott Beale reports he just received a free computer with Windows Vista loaded on it. Now THAT is my idea of Pay Per Post!"

Unlike Zheng, Scoble had a huge audience, and all hell broke loose after that. Within 24 hours, most major bloggers had taken a stand on the issue. Some accused others of a lack of transparency and of accepting payola. Others turned against Microsoft, accusing them of crass pay-per-post schemes. The major news outlets caught wind of the whole mess and started producing their own stories about it. It was now public, and everyone was provoking everyone else.

The whole campaign blew up in our faces. Every time we thought it couldn't get worse, an email would show up and prove that yes, in fact, it could. Edelman sent out a second letter, hoping to calm the storm. It read like a retraction and asked bloggers to either give away the laptop or send it back. Ultimately, it only served to compound the problem. The entire promotion had turned into a car wreck.

Then the tension started to break. In one of the better examples of its self-policing tendencies, the blogosphere started hammering out a new code of conduct for disclosure of company-supplied benefits (now termed "consideration" by the US Federal Trade Commission). If a blogger gets something from a company, he or she should tell readers about it was received and why. This allows bloggers to review products in a timely manner while letting readers make their own judgments about possible conflicts of interest.

Once the madness subsided, the three of us started to realize we had just gotten a massive dose of publicity for AMD and Vista out of the whole snafu. Bloggers being bloggers, they couldn't help but add their 10 cents on the whole issue, and every time they did, AMD and Vista got another mention. Traffic spiked for virtually all the sites involved in the controversy—and by extension, traffic spiked for all those posts and reviews about AMD's notebooks and Microsoft's new operating system. From a publicity standpoint, the whole project worked exceedingly well despite itself—and it all went down just as Vista was about to hit the market. Plus, Acer Ferrari notebooks (the ones most mentioned in the controversy) had huge sales spikes after Christmas.

Somehow, Microsoft and AMD had survived the car wreck—and maybe even come out a little bit ahead. Still, the three of us were jolted enough to make damn sure we knew where we'd made a wrong turn in the whole contorted process. And we were going to make *damn sure* we didn't do the same thing again.

Time To Do It Right

Everyone was flying by the seat of their pants during the Vista campaign. In today's market, a few companies are starting to develop more robust and mature approaches to social media and the marketing opportunities those channels provide. But when we at Ivy Worldwide look at today's online word-of-mouth marketing campaigns, we still see far too many companies just trying anything.

These days, the world of online word-of-mouth marketing has gone mainstream, and a genuine infrastructure and sense of etiquette have formed around it. In fact, an informal but generally accepted code of behavior has settled across the blogosphere. Additionally, the Word of Mouth Marketing Association offers a comprehensive code of ethics (the WOMMA Code of Ethics[1]) to help guide companies who opt to disseminate their messages through social media. This was needed because for many corporations, social-media tools are becoming the new Web page—once a nice add-on but now an indispensible avenue for reaching customers and affecting their perceptions to benefit the business. It's now commonplace—almost expected—to find a company with a Facebook page, a ratings and reviews page, a corporate blog, and a Twitter feed. US federal regulators have even introduced a formal code of conduct for companies and bloggers in hopes of curbing misleading reviews and maintaining a higher level of transparency.

Needless to say, the government's involvement generates its own controversy. But it also serves as a useful reminder that

[1] See: http://womma.org/ethics/code/

online marketing is no longer stuck in its infancy. The practice is maturing, and companies will have to learn, adjust, and make it work for them—or risk being surpassed by competitors who already do. No longer will a brand get credit for merely participating in the online conversation. No longer will people notice a product because it has a neat little Facebook page and nothing else. As the use of social-media tools moves deeper and deeper into mainstream marketing practices, companies will have to do it better if they want to achieve real bottom-line results in this noisy environment.

We've seen too many marketers pat themselves or employees on the back for social-media programs that barely worked or worked only when measured by some meaningless metric that did nothing for the business. An online word-of-mouth marketing campaign won't succeed anymore just because it's *there*. The days of the Wild West are gone, and the luck of the draw has been replaced by online marketing's new marksmen. These marksmen expect a more orderly environment, a safer approach—and one that's more structured—but above all, they now expect *meaningful results*.

Before we launched Ivy Worldwide, the three of us put a lot of good work into the Vista launch, but part of its success was dumb luck. It generated much more buzz, albeit some negative, because of the confusion and controversy that surrounded it. But we can't rely on dumb luck or just "showing up" anymore, and neither can companies looking to extend their messages through social media. Today, Ivy's aim is accurate and precise because the three of us learned from our past mistakes and successes, and those critical lessons now form the core of our philosophy for online word-of-mouth marketing.

Marketers can't keep trying to succeed via the "we'll push out the message, and you'll take it (like it or not)" or the "build it and they will come and buy" approach to word-of-mouth marketing. To succeed as Ivy Worldwide has, marketing professionals need to adopt a new philosophy and, above all, a fundamental shift in mindset that can't be faked or halfhearted in its application. We'll dive into many of our online marketing programs in the following chapters, including several of our most successful campaigns, to give you real-world, proven insight on what to avoid and to shed light on *what works*. But reading these case studies without first understanding the philosophy underpinning them is useless, like walking into a match with a judo expert while knowing all the right moves but not knowing how or when to use them, so let's start with what we believe:

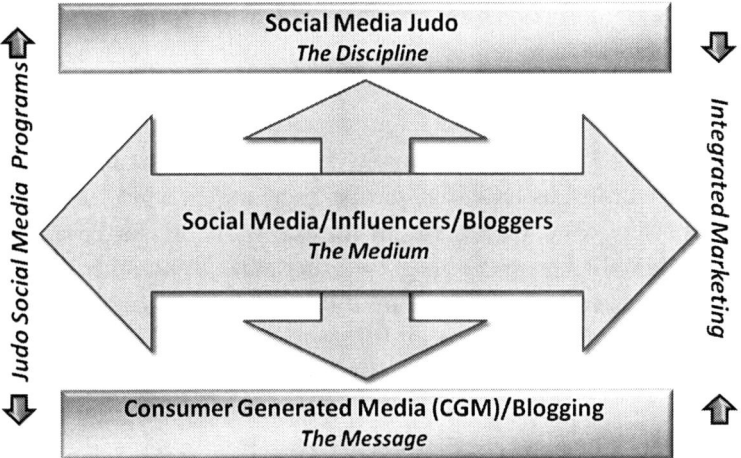

The terms and relationships between the elements of Social Media Judo.

Maximum Outcome From Minimum Effort

It seems simple enough, but simply joining the conversation isn't enough anymore. Many companies try one campaign on Facebook or Twitter, get a couple thousand followers, and pop the champagne. Social media includes dozens of different avenues and approaches. You can't just drive down one block and assume you've reached all your potential customers. Instead, you need to know how to get from A to B as quickly and efficiently as possible. As more of your competitors look to social media to promote their products, your success will depend on getting even closer to the right bloggers, content producers, and social-media avenues to engage to get the best bang for your buck. Why bloggers? Simply put, they've proven to be the most efficient route time and time again. For all the democratic grassroots beauty of the blogosphere, only a relative handful of people really hold sway over opinions about the products and services a company peddles. By reaching out to those content producers, or "influencers," a company can drive meaningful business metrics and, if doing things right, create a sustainable competitive advantage for your product and brand.

Oddly enough, efficiency seems to be a success criterion that many companies overlook, or even fail to recognize, as being relevant and important. For companies long stuck in traditional modes of marketing, working with influencers to spread a message can be a daunting task. Far too many companies either demand perpetually tight-fisted control of their message or just assume that getting anything on a blog, no matter the size, tone, placement, or impact to the business is a win. The mentality seems to be "If we don't make it, or control it, or both, we have not marketed anything." This misses the fundamental point: things are so different now that the usual "just get it done" approach is not only ineffective but can cause significant—and, for that matter, avoidable—harm to your product, brand, business, and career. To put it another way, there's a lot of power wound up in social media and the blogosphere, but misunderstanding ithe dynamics of the social Web is a recipe for disaster. As Nick's high school physics teacher used to say just before he asked someone to try a (usually painful) experiment, "a little knowledge is a dangerous thing."

In the end, we like to use the illustration of judo to give insight into exactly what one is signing up for when looking to spar in social media, as sparring is an apt analogy. For one, the goal is to use the energy and momentum of the online community to serve your social media and influencer marketing goals, much like a judo expert guides his or her opponent with a throw. Similarly, you want to avoid straining against a force that's disinclined to bend to your will. Think of it like guiding

What most executives ask their marketing managers to do. This fire-drill approach leads marketers to just do anything that feels like social media in an effort to put a check mark next to "social media" on their quarterly goals (cartoon by Geek and Poke at http://geekandpoke.typepad.com/geekand poke/2008/04/enterprise-20.html).

the flow of water: You can divert its path with a little effort, but it's a Herculean task to keep it from continuing its flow downstream. When done right, bloggers, influencers, and your customers will take your message wherever they want to go and actually sell on your behalf—with their endorsement for free. Conversely, if you tell your customers, especially your most influential ones, what to think, say, and do, you're bound for nothing but an abrupt, disappointing, and hard fall.

The secret of success is to instead build programs and campaigns that center on what we, at Ivy Worldwide, call the judo effect—building programs using the judo philosophy of minimum effort and maximum results. When used properly, the judo effect enables influencers or bloggers to transparently and credibly sell your product in all the ways *they* want and need to do it for you to be successful. That's the new reality of marketing via social media in the online and offline worlds.

Regrettably, the tendency for most companies is to want to keep a tighter rein on their messages, pushing them out via their own corporate blogs, Twitter feeds, and so on. This misguided effort is understandable and is not a bad thing in and of itself. Take one of today's more popular cases for social media: Dell, Inc. They used social-media tools to engage customers after many of their customers lit up the blogosphere with scathing criticisms of Dell products and customer service. By doing so, Dell started to turn around customer sentiment and transformed some of its loudest and harshest online critics—Jeff Jarvis, in particular—into some of its most ardent supporters. Beyond that, the computer maker claims to have generated millions of dollars in revenue from its Twitter feed and has tens of thousands of followers on its Facebook pages.

The approach worked for Dell, to a certain extent, but the company, for all its online success, has done most of the work internally, pouring an overwhelming amount of money and manpower into those operations. In essence, the company has approached online marketing much like the judo novice, who uses all his energy to defend himself from an attack without actually trying to hit or throw his opponent. We see far too many companies pouring excessive resources into online marketing and getting poor results. The shift in mindset that we espouse instead requires companies to directly engage influencers by partnering with them—or better yet, by co-marketing with them—thus putting into motion a judo move that not only allows but *encourages* real people to sell on the company's behalf.

When companies work with these influencers, the influencers are freed to naturally and credibly take advantage of their networks and conversations to promote your product and brand. Let's be clear: the influencers understand this medium and social media in general far better than many of the marketing managers or "social media experts" working today. They know how to move information and engage audiences to their advantage, ultimately delivering great results for the entire company, be it marketing, sales, support, or design—and at an extremely modest financial and labor expense as compared to what companies normally spend. We know this all sounds too good to be true, but nevertheless, it works, as you will see in the following pages. The key to all of it is to identify the judo move in which you enable the influencers or community to progress into sales, support, design, or any other process (and bear in mind that *you* integrate into *their* processes at the same time). Eventually, you become part of the community, and the community, in turn, helps you achieve your goals—*because it is in their best interest to do so.* We saw it throughout the Vista launch, and we see it today; companies push their word-of-mouth marketing messages without tapping into the momentum already there. They waste too much energy fighting against themselves. For pretty much any company, there's a whole field of influencers and passionate fans online already. You can tap into that power—like a judo expert taps into the energy of his opponent—to get the maximum results with less effort. The judo philosophy has changed the marketing value of our clients' brands, and it can do the same for you and your company.

Mutual Benefit

At AMD, Chris and Geoff often found themselves working in a partner marketing role with larger companies on joint programs, such as with Microsoft during the Vista launch. It didn't take long for the two of them to realize the only successful way to make their ideas see the light of day with these partners was to craft them in a way that made the larger company see the benefit for itself first. As the two of us started working with bloggers, we realized that the same co-marketing principles we used during the Vista launch worked for social media. We got into that mindset, where every day we had to figure out something that would certainly benefit us but would be more clearly and immediately beneficial to our partners first.

When you start talking to influencers, they're open and honest about what they want from a company:

- Be directly and personally engaged.
- Give us content that helps our audiences and drives traffic.
- Stop pushing the same old PR spin or talking points that help only your brand.
- Provide access that helps me generate content my readers can actually use. (This could be a tool, a discount, insight or intelligence, a sneak peek, a solution to a problem, or even just a genuine belly laugh, but it has to matter for it to be of any consequence.)

Companies still stuck in the traditional mindset say, "This is our message, and this is what we want you to do with it." What self-respecting blogger would want to post anything if it didn't truly benefit his or her site and readers? It's been said before, but it bears repeating: These are people, not targets or tools, and they deserve to be treated as such.

At Ivy Worldwide, we call this "customer co-marketing." It defines an approach that's really the fundamental lesson we gleaned from the Vista experience as well as from all of our programs. At no point in that entire campaign did anyone on our team stop to truly consider what the 128 influencers would need to make the campaign work for them. Never did we contemplate how we could arrange those PC trials in a way that would give the bloggers what they wanted—content and, ultimately, traffic. We thought only about how we would get the reviews and good buzz that we wanted for our brand. The infamous letters from Edelman compounded the problem, but by going in with the wrong approach, we limited our ultimate potential from the outset.

To carry off a marketing campaign worthy of a judo master—one that derives the maximum success from the most efficient effort—a company must learn to craft a program that benefits influencers as much as, perhaps even more than, the company itself. This means that you, the marketing manager, must ask the influencers you've targeted at least a few questions before launching into the campaign. It means you have to set out by building personal relationships with these bloggers and content producers—the people who can influence hundreds, thousands, or millions of your customers. It means coming to influencers with your mind open and their needs in mind first, and demonstrating that at every turn—and it must offer these bloggers and your online partners a way to promote themselves, their expertise, and their value to their audiences. If your approach doesn't provide these things first and foremost, your conversation with these influencers—and, by extension, your conversation with your customers—will dry up pretty quickly. Despite the clamor about tips and tricks for word-of-mouth marketing—some of it valuable, much of it not—most companies still overlook this fundamental philosophy, which is critical for consistent success with word-of-mouth campaigns. Every brand wants a cadre of evangelists who can help sway millions of readers with product reviews, blog posts, videos, tweets, and what have you, but the only way to do that is to allow influencers the necessary space to make up their own minds, post what they believe, and adopt your message as their own. They might not give you a glowing review for your latest product, but by establishing a track record and relationship with your key influencers, you can get valuable feedback for your product development, support processes, and marketing cycles—every part of your marketing engine. Besides, bloggers—like anyone, really—are less likely to trash a company they know and trust and if they like the people there.

Consider this actual email pitch from Visa sent to several well-known bloggers:

> *Hi there! My name is [Jane Doe] and I love the forums on your site [BLOG NAME HERE]. I think your forums really stand out as an engaging online community and it seems like your members could definitely be interested in a new online shopping tool that is being introduced. This new tool could help members of your community who shop for the coolest new gadgets online, and may need help comparing products, getting opinions on their finds, and more.*
>
> *Visa is launching a new online shopping tool called Rightcliq™ that brings together the shopping experience to one place – from organizing your purchases to getting advice, from saving money to faster checkout on merchant sites. We are currently in the early product research phase and really want to know what people like you and the members of the [BLOG NAME HERE] community think about it. Can you help us out? We'd like to start a thread about Rightcliq™, have the members of the [BLOG NAME HERE] community give it a try, and give us honest feedback.*
>
> *You can find out more about the service at right-cliq.visa.com. We are only reaching out to a few communities and would love to work with you. Please let me know if you are interested and of course I'd be happy to answer any questions.*

Besides the completely generic email—and that's difficult enough to overlook—there is *absolutely nothing* of any benefit provided to the blogger here. The company wants to post in the bloggers' forums, not even extending the bloggers the opportunity to try out the service and thereby garner a third-party endorsement. Any company-controlled marketing and sales pitch will have an immediately destructive impact on a decent forum, as a marketing communiqué is inherently not about dialogue. The best forums feed off the interaction between real people sharing their thoughts, asking questions, and giving advice. Every blogger knows that a company-controlled thread would kill that interpersonal dynamic in mere milliseconds. Unfortunately, very few companies seem to understand this, as evidenced above. In this case, the company essentially wants to poach the readers of the forum and take over a portion of the site, replacing it with their own information and message. Again we ask, *Why would any self-respecting blogger or influencer want to promote something like that?*

What's more, from the standpoint of a professional marketer, this email shows a remarkable absence of understanding about how marketers ought to work with the momentum of the blogosphere. There's nothing about this effort of Visa's that seems designed to generate any real, measurable, and mutually beneficial results. It's akin to a judo student swinging wildly with his eyes closed and yelling, "I'm going to try to hit you now," and wondering why he did not connect.

To see the difference between this approach and one that could actually amount to meaningful results for marketer and blogger alike, a marketer guided by the *social media judo* mindset would have designed this program with the influencers in mind from the start. A couple of simple yet significant changes could have shifted this effort from being the butt of blogger jokes to a genuine judo success:

1. Visa should have asked the bloggers to be in on the beta test of the service before its launch (not pretending that it is still in beta and trying to steal readers away from the bloggers' sites), giving them the chance to refine the system from the beginning and thus making them part of the team. The influencers could then claim credit to their readers for the product they helped build while simultaneously endorsing it—which, of course, they would do, as *they helped build the thing.*

2. This is a shopping site, so apparently Visa understands that people go to blogs for product advice; however, Visa failed to offer to link to the discussion on the bloggers' forums and thus drive a reciprocal relationship that shares traffic between the two. In other words, Visa had the opportunity to help the blogger generate content for his site and at the same time help populate the site with inbound links from Visa—this could have been a very enticing proposition for the blogger. But Visa didn't do this.

3. Furthermore, Visa should have provided something of long-term value to the bloggers, thereby creating an implicit ongoing dialogue with them. A promotional contest run by the bloggers with prizes for their readers, or deals exclusive to the bloggers' communities, or anything else that would enable the bloggers to promote the new service (or all of the above) would have given these influential bloggers an active stake in promoting the new shopping service.

Instead, Visa chose what we call a drive-by approach and elicited a commensurate response from the bloggers, not to mention, Visa probably didn't achieve any goals that actually translated into meaningful business metrics for its business. But then again, Visa very likely saw any neutral reaction as a success and moved on, as so lamentably many marketers tend to do in today's social-media arena.

Had Visa employed social media judo, it could have accomplished truly consequential business objectives, but its lack of understanding of the following key concepts spelled failure from the start.

1. Successful bloggers are some of the best online marketers in the world—they have to be if they want to get hundreds of thousands, even millions, of readers coming back every month. Tapping into the bloggers'

expertise would've helped Visa create a campaign that created reams of content that engaged the audience in a way that Visa clearly does not understand.

2. If bloggers are part of the process and their content is being used as an integral part of Visa's program, they then have a vested interest in promoting Visa's message on their blogs and to their communities, forums, Twitter followers, YouTube subscribers, and so on.

3. When Visa promotes the bloggers and their content on Visa's site, the company helps drive traffic to the bloggers. This in turn makes the bloggers more valuable to Visa and Visa more valuable to the bloggers, creating a virtuous cycle—not to mention, all including the bloggers' invaluable third-party endorsement of the product or service

This is the beauty of the judo approach. With a few small steps, we can transform a poorly conceived campaign and lousy email pitch into a true and credible influencer-marketing campaign capable of delivering real results to the business while also driving traffic and increasing time on-site. The company will give up some measure of control in the process, but in so doing, it will gain evangelists who will promote the site and the brand today and tomorrow while transferring an invaluable third-party endorsement that drives sales.

Still, we know the move from traditional to social media marketing is a difficult transition for most companies, as it forces marketers out of their comfort zones and into building long-lasting relationships with influential voices. For us at Ivy Worldwide, working with influential bloggers in this way is really the best part of our job. When Chris and Geoff left AMD to start Ivy Worldwide, it meant no more asinine press releases and talking points, all of which bloggers hate more than you will ever know (yes, even the "social-media press releases").

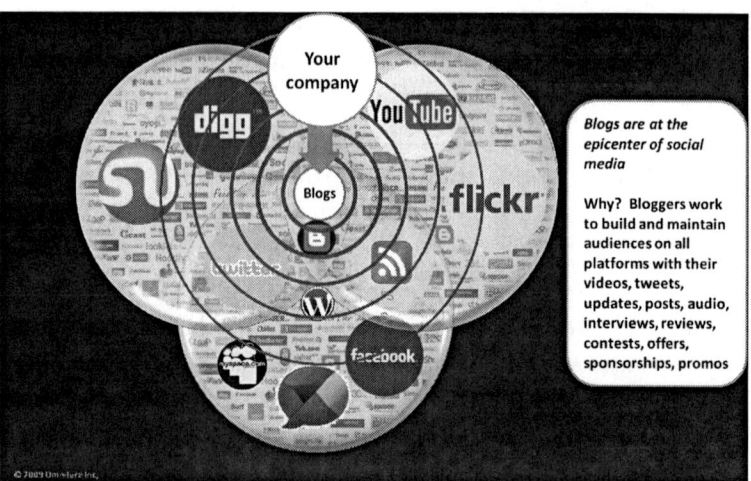

Bloggers are the key drivers of social media and are experts at online marketing. This chart from Omniture shows how they have become the epicenter of social media.

In many respects, we were lucky when we launched what became Ivy Worldwide. We were free to do what works and to engage with really bright, influential people. And when Nick left Microsoft to join Chris and Geoff, we pieced together one of the largest Rolodexes of online content producers out there. We know them; they know and trust us.

Many of these influencers have a voice throughout this book. We made sure they did because they have interesting stories to tell about the (sometimes baffling) range of marketing programs that companies bring to them. But we also include their insight because they're the experts on social media and word-of-mouth marketing. We don't feature them because we like them, although we do; we feature them because they're the experts in engaging an audience and this is something we have learned from and you should too. Plus, every day, they talk to the people your company is trying to reach. And every day, they get those people to act and buy.

CHAPTER 1

Social-Media Marketing

IF YOU'RE A GEEK, YOU probably know Chris Pirillo. He is one of the Web's leading technology influencers and the driving force behind both Lockergnome and chris.pirillo.com. Millions of tech enthusiasts visit his sites, watch his videos, or read his posts every month. The Gnomedex conference he founded, entering its 10th year in 2010, has become one of the can't-miss annual events for the blogosphere.

Pirillo has a massive audience across all his ventures, and consistently providing quality content for all those communities keeps him hopping, so he's a great example of why the judo philosophy is so vital for companies that want to generate word-of-mouth buzz across the Internet. By simply tapping into Pirillo's vast audience and expertise, a company can spread its message to millions of potential customers at once, but no company will get through his virtual door without offering him something in return. "They're asking me for my time, my expertise, my audience," he says. "You're asking me to do a lot and most of it does nothing for my readers."

At Ivy Worldwide, we've worked on a few campaigns with Chris, including a couple we put together for HP. It's hard to pass up an audience that large, and we know we need to bring something to the table to make it worth Chris's while, but we can't and don't reserve this approach for only big fish like Chris Pirillo or Xavier Lanier, who founded the Notebooks.com family of Web sites. For a company that adopts the judo philosophy, this fundamental give-and-take becomes a key piece of any online marketing campaign. Successful companies will craft campaigns in which the effort needed to participate produces results that are as valuable for the influencers as they are for the brand. "Rarely does one size fit all," Lanier says. "It's kind of like herding cats with bloggers. They all have their own approach, and there's not one way to approach an audience across different geographies and demographics. So instead of coming to us and saying, 'We want you to promote our company,' it's important for companies to offer value to the whole community, not just the blogger as the community leader."

Let's be clear, though: None of this is meant to suggest a pay-per-post approach. Providing value to the entire community means giving influencers like Pirillo, Lanier, and others the content they need to engage their communities and help them drive traffic. It means providing appropriate access to products and people so influencers can credibly and transparently talk about our clients' brands. It means giving something that benefits the influencers as much as it benefits the company. And it means giving them the flexibility to present all that content—whether a giveaway, a review, or a piece of technical analysis—in the way that best fits their audience. After all, the influencers have already proven their ability to reach your market and get its members to act or buy. Why would you want to get in the way of that and risk removing or losing their endorsement?

When we do social media programs properly, the influencers will promote our clients' brands because doing so helps them drive traffic to their sites. It's why we go out of our way to build personal relationships with influencers across the Web; we try to help them as much as we help any of our clients, and in turn they help us. In fact, taking an active interest in the influencers' success means we create an interpersonal relationship with them, and we can lean on that when it's necessary to do so. It also means that influencers gain access to the companies and brands in a way that helps improve their influence with their audience, making the interactions between bloggers, Ivy Worldwide, and our clients more effective with each successive engagement. Take a minute to search for our names via your favorite search engine and you'll see from what other people say about us that this is true. We're proud of the comments that influencers have gone out of their way to post about us, and we have built personal relationships with hundreds of key influencers to make that happen. We also work hard to craft marketing campaigns that will benefit influencers as much as they benefit our clients. We came to them from the start with our hands and heads open, asking them to tell us what would work best. By approaching influencers as friends with a desire to help instead of as targets that we intend to exploit, we're able tap into their influence in a way that delivers maximum results for all, with a minimum of effort.

We place this judo philosophy at the core of everything we do. Instead of overpowering an opponent, the judo master will use his foe's momentum against him. Rather than waste all our effort trying to force a client's message out across the blogosphere, we work with site publishers to leverage their existing influence and reach the millions of potential customers they talk with every day. We took the approach that we researched for this book. Who better to educate us about the sport than Neil Ohlenkamp, an expert teacher in Southern California who founded and runs one of the most popular judo-related sites on the Web, www.JudoInfo.com? Do a search for the term "judo," and Ohlenkamp's site is perched among the top results, higher than for the associations that govern the sport.

Ohlenkamp said he started the site on a lark, as a way to help teach more people about the sport he loved. In the years since, the site has become the perfect allegory for his passion. Ohlenkamp tapped the power of the Internet and social media, and did it in a way that allowed him to spread the word on judo further and to more people than did most of the country's top judo associations. Just as a judo expert uses the momentum of his or her opponent, Ohlenkamp used the Internet and social media to reach a broader audience through less effort. We do the same. It's possible for a social-media marketing campaign to ride the existing flow already available online—one just has to understand the dynamic at the core of the flow to be able to do so. (The same is true of judo.) People are talking about your brand right now, today, and by tapping into that momentum, you can help amplify your message.

Companies that learn how to best work with these key influential voices will produce consistently stronger results from their online marketing campaigns while consistently spending less, but it takes a mindset focused on mutual benefit and requires the right strategies, processes, and tools. And when everything comes together, it can produce spectacular results. Even with all the right intentions, however, none of this works without an understanding how word of mouth is evolving and how social media is taking it in new directions.

A cartoon from Chris Pirillo and Brad Fitzpatrick at Blaugh.com illustrating that if the influencers are not talking about your product or brand, you are, in essence, irrelevant (see: http://blaugh.com/2007/02/13/if-a-blog-falls/).

The Evolution Of Word Of Mouth

The instant humans evolved into a verbal species, word of mouth became the most powerful tool for spreading a message. It organized the first coordinated hunts. It propagated knowledge of concepts like fire and tools. It spread the teachings of the world's religions. And when people started bartering their handiwork to others, it became the most powerful tool in business marketing—and it remains so today.

Asa Candler understood this better than most business owners of the late 19th century. Candler purchased the formula for Coca-Cola in 1887. The world's most popular soft drink now, Coke had very little following when Candler got his hands on the formula. He set out to change that.

Candler began distributing coupons for free Cokes, initially sending them by direct mail to potential customers. According to Phil Mooney, an archivist and historian for Coca-Cola, about 8.5 million coupons were redeemed between 1894 and 1913 – about one coupon for every nine U.S. citizens at the time.. In 1905, Candler advertised in *Good Housekeeping*, *Munsey's*, and *Scribner's* magazines, with a coupon at the bottom of each advertisement. By the end of the year, customers had redeemed almost $43,000 worth of coupons, Mooney writes on his blog, www.coca-colaconversations.com.

But Candler also made sure he kept his partners in mind, too. He provided them coupons to give to their best customers, who could then try a Coke at the shop's soda fountain. He figured taking a hit on one Coke would capture customers and help them encourage their friends and neighbors to buy the soft drink again and again and again, but he also realized that generating business for those merchants—his distributors at the time—ultimately meant more business for him. Make them happy, and they'd push more Coke—and that, of course, made him happy.

It's a remarkable story of judo marketing, although Candler probably never thought about it in those terms. What he knew—and what remains true today—is that word of mouth remains the most powerful force available to marketers today. Rather than try to shout above the din to get everyone's attention, Candler tapped into the quickly widening array of fans and distributors who were happy to help spread the word credibly and honestly, with better results than he could achieve via traditional marketing. Even now, however, centuries after humans started talking and more than a century after Candler built Coke into a household brand, word of mouth remains the least understood and, far too often, least utilized form of marketing.

To some degree, part of the word-of-mouth phenomenon will stay a little hazy. What someone tells a neighbor or friend about his or her new riding lawnmower might depend on any number of variables. In his seminal book, *Word of Mouth Marketing*, Andy Sernovitz calls this organic word of mouth. That organic world of mouth is extremely valuable. It derives of itself, the quality of your brand, and the quality of your products, and it typically carries a very high degree of authority. Now, thanks in large part to the megaphone known as the Internet, organic word of mouth can spread faster and farther than ever before. That amplifying effect has spurred more and more companies to try to build a marketing component around the online word-of-mouth idea. Sernovitz labels this as amplified word of mouth, which "is started by an intentional campaign to get people talking."

With the rapid and broad spread of information on the blogosphere today, ignorance of either organic or amplified word of mouth poses a real threat to your brand's image and your company's success. As recently as a decade ago, if someone didn't like your product, he or she might complain to a dozen people, who might each in turn tell a handful of others, and that was about the extent of the bad vibe. Today, an unsatisfied customer blogs about it and you risk ending up with an online wildfire on your hands. Then your CEO finds out and orders you, the unhappy brand manager, to contain it.

Oh, if it were only so simple to contain it. Not only does word-of-mouth spread like a virus in this Web-mediated world, but this world also charges a new premium for authenticity and credibility. And that's not something you can build overnight whenever something goes wrong (and they *do* go wrong). Consumers and bloggers have a new veto power over corporate America and the great marketing machine. Consumers and bloggers now initiate, direct, and control the conversation in ways that didn't exist just a few years ago. As a result, companies now have to talk *with* their customers, not *at* them. "Here's the thing: Your marketing message is still your marketing message, but the reaction to it is much more public now," says Xavier Lanier, founder of Notebooks.com. "You definitely have less control in terms of reaction, but that's all the more reason to involve your biggest proponents beforehand."

Authenticity And Authority

Online and traditional word-of-mouth campaigns share the same goal: Get customers to take your message and make it their own. As Lanier notes, a company can put out its message, and that will remain the company's message (with all the good and bad that that entails). When customers start spreading the message in their own words, though, the message takes on a whole new level of authority—authority that, *by definition*, cannot be replicated by the company or the brand. That was true with Coke when Candler was distributing his coupons at the turn of the 20th century, and it remains so now. But these days, the online evangelist on the proverbial (albeit virtual) street corner is now shouting loudly enough for practically anyone in the Web-connected world to hear it.

Jackie Huba and Ben McConnell offer a thoughtful discussion of the authority third parties bring to a marketing message in their popular book, *Citizen Marketers: When People Are the Message*. Influential messages need to have some degree of authenticity—the more, the better. Nothing adds more authority to a message than authenticity, and for most consumers, nothing is less authentic than the gears of the corporate machine. The most authentic, and thus more authoritative, messages come from someone you trust: a friend, a family member, a respected colleague, and as more of those trusted acquaintances share the same advice, the message gains ever more authority and momentum.

"A distinct advantage citizen marketers hold over many traditional media is what we call 'dynamic authority,'" Huba and McConnell write. "It is the authority fueled by a continuous, productive activity." Their thinking makes perfect sense, especially as they take it another step. If a message created and sent forth by a company carries less authenticity, and if authority grows from authenticity, then it follows that it would behoove a company to work with customers who can provide that "continuous and productive activity." Consider the lifestyle associated with Harley-Davidson motorcycles. A friend of ours once called Harley riders a "mobile billboard" for the company. Few businesses can boast the kind of brand loyalty that Harley-Davidson can. You see someone riding a Hog, and a set of very distinct associations comes to mind—rough-and-tumble riders, masters of their own domain who're free to cruise the open road. Virtually all of those riders have taken the Harley mystique and made it their own. They've taken the Harley brand message and put it into their own words. Each time they get on their Harleys or put on their leather vests with the Harley-Davidson logo, they create a much more dynamic authority for the brand than the brand could ever hope to create for itself.

Imagine, then, a world where Harley could send one of its bikes rumbling down every street on the planet—or, perhaps more fittingly, down your street just as you were mulling about how fun it would be to own a motorcycle. Word-of-mouth marketing, when done properly, can send your product down the right social media avenues at precisely the right time, reaching out through influencers online to arrive at the virtual doorsteps of millions of customers—and arriving just when those customers are thinking about the need that your product fulfills. Ten years ago, dynamic authority like this came from organic word of mouth amongst individuals, or by way of a story in the newspaper. Today, it comes from influencers— voices with reach, authority, and credibility—posting their views and opinions on blogs, Facebook, Twitter, and all the other social media outlets scattered throughout the Internet. They will produce that dynamic authority for your brand, but it's up to you to make it easy and convenient for them to do so.

"31 Days Of The Dragon"

In more ways than we could possibly realize at the time, Ivy Worldwide's success was set in motion by three largely unrelated events in the spring of 2007. Those events would set up one of the most successful and multiple-award-winning online marketing campaigns ever produced.

Around April 2007, Advanced Micro Devices (AMD) wrapped up a joint online marketing program with HP to help bolster the launch of HP's new TX1000 tablet PC. We had decided to seed 20 of the systems with bloggers to see what sort of buzz we could generate about them. To be fair, given all the other marketing and PR campaigns involved in the launch of the TX1000, we can't say with 100% certainty that our plan prompted the big uptick that hit the product's sales, but when we looked at the wave of positive buzz generated by the reviews that those 20 bloggers posted, we knew we'd hit a sweet spot.

That would be the last major marketing campaign Chris and Geoff did at AMD. In April 2007, they left the company to form Buzz Corps (renamed to Ivy Worldwide in 2009). In fact, our decision to leave AMD was born from the success of the TX1000 campaign, as the bloggers were encouraging us to help other companies "get it" the way AMD did. We had seen the vast and untapped potential of word-of-mouth marketing long before this point, but we'd not taken this decisive, irrevocable step. Now it was all laid out before us and the choice was more than clear. To have experienced what's possible via word-of-mouth marketing and then have someone tell us to write *yet another meaningless press release*—well, the chance to strike out on our own was just too tempting to pass up. As a result, our agency was born, and the second crucial, serendipitous event had come to pass.

Around the time we were getting our business up and running, the third key event was occurring halfway around the world. At a mobile computing event in Shanghai, HP was launching 13 new notebook computers, including a monster of a machine it called the Pavilion HDX Dragon. The Dragon was a fire-snorting beast of a home-entertainment PC: it boasted a 20-inch screen, the top-of-the-line processor, and all the latest bells and whistles you'd expect to go along with a PC of this caliber—and all for a cool $5,000. This was HP's new flagship machine. Later that year, Craig Simms would review it for CNet Australia: "HP's Pavilion HDX is quite possibly the best 'because we can' item that we've seen in a while—but for those who don't mind dabbling on the luxury side, it's a must-buy item."

HP pulled out all the traditional marketing stops to support the launch of the HDX Dragon, but by the end of the year, sales were limping along. "Sales were doing OK but not great," said Scott Ballantyne, then the Vice President and General Manager of HP's Personal Systems Group, but for a flagship product—one that was supposed to create a halo effect for sales of all other products in the HP portfolio—the HDX Dragon wasn't generating nearly enough interest. By the end of the year, sales were pretty well flat and the early buzz had all but faded.

HP rarely engaged social media at the time, and rival computer makers were starting to steal the company's thunder with their own social-media efforts. Dana Harrold, one of HP's marketing managers at the time, remembered the success we had shared when generating buzz for the TX1000 tablet PC. She picked up the phone and gave us a call. HP's traditional marketing for the Dragon had run its course, so Harrold needed to try something new to sustain and expand the halo effect around the flagship notebook. We set out three goals to meet HP's need:

- Give back to the community that had built relationships with HP and helped promote the products
- Drive awareness and sales of the Dragon and HP PCs overall
- Turn the table on competitors who were making a bigger splash through social media

As a technology company, HP clearly needed to deepen its commitment to the blogosphere. It needed to show a new level of support for the kinds of social media initiatives that had built strong relationships between the company and its key influencers and customers. After all, many of the most influential bloggers on the Internet were clamoring for better access to the company and its products. The situation called for a firm that could bring those two sides together—between our relationships and HP's desire to move the needle, the fit couldn't have been better.

Ivy Worldwide is "coming at social media from a formerly corporate perspective, which is helpful when you're bridging between publishers and a corporate entity," said Chris Pirillo. "In an ideal world, corporations shouldn't need a translator, but corporations' needs are different from publishers' needs. ... [A] corporation tends to devalue a publisher in many, many ways." Companies badly want to get in front of an online publisher's audience, he said, but they won't usually push forward to build a personal relationship with their influencers. What's more, companies rarely understand influencers' needs, so they don't know how to provide anything of real value for the influencers' audience.

We'd already made it a point to get to know influencers like Pirillo on both personal and professional levels, so it was hardly remarkable when he called to ask whether we had anything he could give away to his readers. It's a common request from online publishers—after all, they have an audience to appease, engage, and expand. A little freebie once in a while tends to help on all fronts. The remarkable part about his call, though, was the timing: It happened to come right around the time that Harrold had called about jumpstarting the HDX Dragon marketing campaign. It got us thinking: Why not give away a $5,000 computer instead of just another mouse? In fact, why don't we give away a bunch of the Dragons? What should keep us from giving away something absolutely *enormous*?

We initially suggested that HP run a program over 20 days, with a different blogger giving away a fully loaded Dragon system each of those days. They ran it up the flagpole, and after more brainstorming and some feedback from both HP and the bloggers, we jointly decided to expand the program to cover an entire month. Thus, 31 Days of the Dragon was born.

Making It Work

Before we go too far, we need to stress two critical elements we had to establish before 31 Days of the Dragon could get off the ground. First, every influencer had to agree to promote and link to the other 30, and each had to agree to give the systems away on a randomly assigned date. By doing that, the interlinked contests would generate a wave of attention across all those sites, building traffic for each one and vaulting the HDX Dragon to the top of many search engine rankings. HP, in contrast, had to agree to stay out of the way, letting the bloggers give away the Dragon in any way they chose. By doing so, HP let the bloggers get creative in structuring their contests, which in turn allowed readers to get creative with the content they generated for the contests. (As an added bonus—one that HP very much liked—gifting the PCs to the bloggers and then putting the contest into their hands removed all the legal and managerial red tape that HP would've had to deal with if it ran the contest in-house.)

Once we put 31 Days in motion, we worried most about how other influencers would react to being left out. After all, there was no possible way to include everyone who'd want to be part of this program. But we saw no backlash, in part because those who weren't included saw the program as a positive step for the blogosphere as a whole. In addition, many of them called us to ask if we'd consider including them in another program next time around, rather than deciding to rail against us and HP online. It's no secret that bloggers and their readers are notorious for finding the fly in the soup, and we wanted to make sure that this broth was pristine. It came down to our ability to understand the world that bloggers and their audiences (i.e., HP's customers) operate in. Luckily, that's precisely what we do.

And of course, the bloggers did what bloggers do. The 31 influencers started writing about the contest, the HDX Dragon, HP in general, and each other. It turned into an unprecedented cyclone of grassroots marketing, and one that ended up as a clear illustration of the collective power that can amass when a community bands together in a way that's mutually beneficial to everyone involved. The bloggers worked together to create shared marketing materials, a microsite, graphics, logos, RSS feeds, videos, and the like, then they cross-promoted those items with one another. Each influencer created his or her own unique contest, in many cases designed to drive traffic to a new venture he or she was launching (such as a new brand, forum, or YouTube channel).We let each influencer tailor the promotion to his or her exact audience and goal. Including the pre- and post-content coverage, HP enjoyed more than 45 days of positive discussion about its business and its flagship HDX Dragon PC. The buzz spawned huge lists of third-party endorsements—a giant dose of the critical "dynamic authority" that Huba and McConnell explain in their book.

Showing the power of consumer-generated content, word-of-mouth marketing and social media all at once, influencer Chris Pirillo's numerous videos
were watched by millions of consumers and included viewers praising the
HDX and HP in his scrolling comment window.

31 Days Of The Dragon's Business Impact

HP could not have bought 31 Days' results with traditional
media spending. Readers created videos to enter several of the
bloggers' giveaways, generating more than 10 million views
from consumers who watched them. Pirillo alone produced
videos watched by millions of consumers, and his readers
posted hundreds of comments on his scrolling video chat log,
most praising the HDX Dragon and HP. The buzz was tremendous, *and it carried over to sales.* HPShopping.com immediately
saw

- 84% month-on-month increase in sales on the HDX
Dragon system

- Overall traffic to HP's shopping site increased by 14%
- A 10% jump from seasonal and monthly figures for over-all consumer PC sales during the month
- The company set several records for monthly sales fig-ures even before the high-volume, back-to-school time-frame, and those gains stuck even months after the program ended

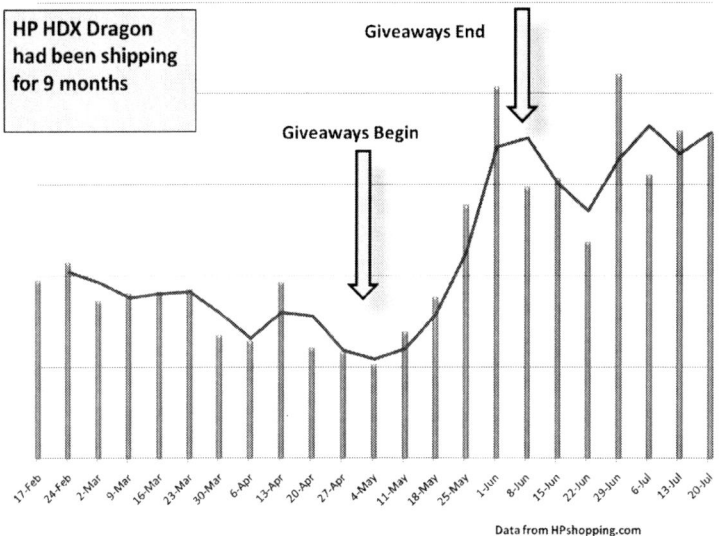

Data from HPshopping.com

Sales data for 31 Days of the Dragon showing the impact and continued growth for a product that had been shipping for 9 months before the pro-motion (data provided by HPshopping.com).

Even better, all those gains came at minimal cost. HP's total outlay for the computers, shipping, software, Ivy Worldwide's fee, and payments to offset taxes for contest winners totaled $250,000. That's all but pocket change for results of this mag-nitude for a company the size of HP, and in the end, HP paid $0—nada, zilch, nothing—for media advertising or to the 31 influencers who participated in the program.

31 Days of the Dragon – Results

Business advances, sales gains, increased product awareness and competitive advantage

Results from HPshopping.com (month over month data)
- 84% increase in sales on the HDX Dragon system
- 14% increase in overall traffic
- 10% increase in overall consumer PC sales
- Sales figures for the month of the program set several records
- The sales gains continued even months after the program

Costs
- Total cost for systems, shipping, software and paying to offset taxes for the winners: $250K (costs shared by HP and partners)
- $0 media spend – and we did not pay the influencers

Results from 31 Days of the Dragon

But none of this could have happened if HP hadn't let the content producers get their piece as well. We polled the 31 influencers after the campaign and learned that their traffic increased anywhere from 150% to 5,000% during the promotion. Even better, those new readers kept coming back. The sites *averaged* a 50% traffic increase two months later. The bloggers also forged a deeper relationship with HP; it was not lost on them that HP had given them front-row seats for its largest-ever product launch, which occurred two days after the 31 Days ended.

Because of 31 Days, HP went from a laggard in social media to one of the leaders. The company learned that the online community can work in dynamic ways and bring about disproportionately efficient results that traditional media can't (or won't) offer. Influencers can and will drive sales and create a viral effect for a brand, and as part of a holistic program such as 31 Days, such a supercharged activity forces competitors to become reactive to you taking the lead. Ultimately, 31 Days did more to increase both HP's sales and influencers' traffic than virtually any other online marketing promotion ever, and people noticed. The program won the *Word of Mouth Marketing Association's* Wommy Award for the best campaign of the year. HP presented us with its CIRCLE Award for the company's best overall marketing campaign worldwide. The research firm Aberdeen Group named HP *Best-in-Class for Social Media*. All told, 31 Days won more than a dozen awards for marketing effectiveness.

A small sample of the search results, content, and marketing created by the influencers to promote 31 Days of the Dragon across the Internet. For a full overview on this program, see: http://www.slideshare.net/BuzzCorps/hp-and-buzz-corps-31-days-of-the-dragon-case-study.

Key Takeaways From 31 Days

• Social media marketing can work in ways traditional methods can't or won't

• Influencers can and will drive sales and create a viral effect

• A holistic program such as "31 Days of the Dragon" forces competitors to become reactive to your marketing

• The combination of social media, CGM, search results and third-party endorsement from credible sources created a wall of information that was compelling and virtually unavoidable for potential customers

Key takeaways from 31 Days of the Dragon

The Judo Effect

The 31 Days campaign worked in just about every conceivable way, and it paid off in spades for everyone involved, yet the real beauty of the program came from its network effect: Each influencer brought with him or her an enthusiastic community and shared his or her individual momentum with the 30 other influencers. Each new day would bring another blogger a massive collective group of readers, many of whom stuck around long after the program's end.

As its presence grew, both during and after the execution of 31 Days, the HDX Dragon started dominating search-engine results. You couldn't do a Web search on computers without running into something about HP's flagship laptop. Word of the program also managed to spread through more traditional channels such as email, but it literally exploded through social-media avenues, including other influencers, their communities, and social networking sites such as Facebook and Twitter. We'd created a wave of information so big that it would soak anyone surfing the Web for information about a new PC—and a lot of people who hadn't been looking at all. The wave covered every phase of the consumer purchase-decision cycle: awareness, consideration, trial, adoption, and advocacy.

Bringing about this type of broad and sustained impact has become increasingly vital for companies that want to pull off successful marketing campaigns in today's hypermediated world. Once you go online, news and discussion that's here today is usually gone tomorrow, so the messages that resist this constant turnover are the ones that end up resonating with customers. The changes and challenges go even deeper than marketing, however; the very way that consumers go about making their decisions to buy have evolved, and irrevocably so. McKinsey & Co. released a study[2] that upended the old notion of the traditional "purchase funnel." In the past, consumers became

[2]See: http://www.mckinseyquarterly.com/Marketing/Strategy/The_consumer_decision_journey_2373?gp=1#

36

aware of a set of brands and then narrowed down their choices to a smaller set of brands that they'd consider buying. At that point, should they decide to purchase, they'd settle on a choice and, if all went well, might even end up becoming loyal to one brand in particular. At each successive step, the number of brands in contention would shrink.

In this day and age, however, the shape of the funnel has changed. In fact, the whole process has morphed into something much less linear and much more cyclical. In research that included interviews with almost 20,000 consumers worldwide, McKinsey found that once something triggers a purchase decision, it sets off a cycle that flows in four phases:

1. **Initial consideration** – This is rooted in the ongoing exposure that consumers have to a brand. The exposure occurs every day, through advertising, word of mouth and any number of other online or offline sources. Eventually, though, a trigger goes off that spurs the consumer into action, and these triggers increasingly have an external rather than internal stimulus: I decide to buy a new smartphone because my current contract expires or my old phone dies, not because a new smartphone hits the market (as many marketers are convinced is the case). Note that the key change in this early stage is that the list of brands a consumer considers is *quite narrow*. The traditional model would hold that the broadest possible set of brands is considered during this first phase, and yet with media messages constantly bombarding consumers these days, this initial consideration list is quite short—making it all the more difficult for brands to appear in.

2. **Active evaluation** – Don't worry if you can't get on that short list, because consumers then pass into an active evaluation of the product they intend to buy. It's at this stage that, rather than getting shorter, the list of brands they consider in fact begins to increase. The consumer now is searching the Internet, gathering

information and paying closer attention to advertising and other traditional marketing. Consumer-driven marketing—word-of-mouth, online reviews, and print reviews—has much more influence in this stage than during initial consideration

3. **Closure** – The moment of purchase has arrived. This is a critical point for products in retail, because in many cases consumers still haven't made their final decision and their decision therefore still remains susceptible to influence. [However, in our view, a properly conceived marketing campaign will eliminate much of the uncertainty a consumer might carry into a retail store—or, better still, the campaign will make it easy to purchase online so the consumer can strike while the purchase-decision iron is hot]

4. **The loyalty loop** – Brand loyalty used to be a fairly active trait: A consumer would find a brand he or she liked and would stick to that brand. Today, loyalty has become a more passive affair. People may remain open to repurchase once they've bought, but this pseudo-loyalty doesn't preclude the possibility that they'll consider other brands when they next find themselves in the active evaluation phase. No customer is captive anymore.[3]

We could only nod in vigorous agreement as we read McKinsey's report. After all, we'd seen this phenomenon on display through the 31 Days campaign. The wave of information the promotion had generated put the HDX Dragon on everyone's radar during the initial consideration phase. It provided an overwhelming collection of reviews—by both influencers and their communities—expounding the merits of HP's machine and the brand by extension. It clearly sparked a wave of sales.

---

[3] This excludes brands or products with overwhelming switching costs or other lock-in functions.

How well the campaign retains loyalty to HP remains to be seen, but because more people consider more brands during the active evaluation phase, they can still avail themselves today of the wave of information that the program generated on the Dragon and the stature of HP's brand, including new reviews and ratings from those who own HP systems. With 31 Days, we were able to penetrate all of McKinsey's new consumer-decision stages at precisely the right time. In fact, the messaging was so widespread and the buzz so strong that in many cases, the promotion became *the sole* trigger for consumers who hadn't even planned to buy a new PC until coming across the promotion.

But it bears stating that coverage that broad and deep—extensive enough to cover all the phases comprising a customer's purchasing decision—doesn't come without a little help. A company can usually spark such saturation coverage with a phenomenal product, the kind of product that comes along only once in a few years or every decade. More realistically, generating the same saturation for a merely great product requires too much time, energy, and money to attempt it on your own. Instead, you have to adopt the judo expert's approach: Find ways to use the existing momentum that your company's key influencers already provide. With 31 Days, we did exactly that. We worked with HP to leverage the strength of the network and the influencers' communities to our advantage. We put our effort into creating the first spark of momentum, then got out of the way and let the Internet's inertia take over. We allowed influencers to do what was in their best interest first, knowing that doing so ultimately would provide HP everything it wanted and more. By understanding everyone's motives and goals, we developed a program that delivered significant rewards for all participants.

Let's be clear, though: We didn't abandon the fundamentals of traditional marketing, and neither did we do this as an add-on or standalone aside from all the other work HP's marketing teams had done for the HDX Dragon push. A marketing group still must consider target markets, segmentation, sales strategies, promotions, and all the marketing elements necessary to ensure a real return on investment. To put it another way, social media does not stand on its own but rather is an integral (albeit regularly misunderstood) element in today's marketer's toolkit. For example, we didn't select a huge group of general technology influencers for inclusion in 31 Days; instead, we selected a smallish set of content producers who would have the greatest possible impact on potential HDX Dragon buyers and on PC consumers in general; thus, we selected influencers who directly reached the target market for the Dragon and HP's other notebooks. Think of it like casting a movie: You're going to have a lead actor, supporting characters, extras and so on—a cast that can pull the story together from the required variety of viewpoints.

We certainly don't suggest that companies abandon traditional marketing. In fact, online word-of-mouth marketing has to exist as only a small piece of a larger, fully integrated marketing campaign. We do suggest two things:

1. A new philosophy that starts with word of mouth having equal weight in the marketing mix
2. A new set of skills that connects with today's consumers and influencers for mutual benefit while understanding the changing habits in the decision-making process

As you'll see in upcoming chapters, this new mindset and skill set sound so simple and straightforward, yet they're nevertheless a fundamental departure from the marketing approach of old. Today's successful marketers will find ways to generate maximum efficiency with minimum effort and expense. They'll develop programs that provide mutual satisfaction to the brand and its influencers and customers. They'll learn the new etiquette of the blogosphere, setting out to build personal relationships with key influencers, availing themselves of the influencers' momentum while staying out of their way at the same time. They'll work much more closely with these influencers than they might at first expect, getting inside the influencers' heads and understanding the influencers' needs in the same way marketers are trained to understand the customers' needs. And if they can manage to understand all of this, today's marketers will end up possessing a new set of skills that, instead of causing them to fight gravity and lose their balance in the process, will help them achieve world-class results with mind-bending efficiency.

In short, they'll have taken a lesson from the world's judo masters.

CHAPTER 2

The Judo Philosophy

JUDO MEANS "GENTLE WAY" IN English, which might seem odd to those who stumble across an occasional match during the Olympics. The sport's throws, counters, and grappling appear exceedingly violent at times, yet those who know judo will notice how little effort the experts put forth to create such powerful results. By getting an opponent off balance and harnessing his or her momentum, the expert can get the most spectacular throws to come off with much less effort than a layman would imagine. "There's one uniform realization for judo students that happens when they throw someone effortlessly, and they don't really know how it happened. They just did it," says Neil Ohlenkamp, who has taught the sport for more than 35 years. "It happens to everybody, and when it does they always say, 'Ah-hah! That's judo!' It's sort of just a feeling, but effortlessness is part of it."

On one of the JudoInfo.com forums, a member posted a striking photo of one judo expert throwing another. It caught our eye because it so perfectly revealed judo's contrast of gentleness and violence. In the photo, one of the fighters is a complete blur of motion, while the other fighter is in perfect focus, barely moving.

The photo's stillness represents a perfect combination of the physical and philosophical. Ohlenkamp sees this combination in his judo students as well. As they start to understand the sport as a partnership between the mindset and the physical skill, he says, they stop thrashing around and stay in the

Photo from: http://vkoreanmartialarts.com.

moment. They see opportunities as they arrive, so they don't have to think about what to do, losing valuable time and position. "You have to get to the question of when to apply these things, and the timing of course is critical," Ohlenkamp says about judo. "That's when you have to understand the principle behind that throw. What is it that makes the throw work?"

Virtually every professional athlete goes through the same process; they spend so much time training that actual play or performance becomes all but instinctual. The great athletes turn off their minds and let their bodies react; their reflexes are preprogrammed while remaining flexible enough to adapt to any situation. Rarely does a situation look new to such athletes, and when it does, they have the uncanny ability to break it down and figure it out in an instant.

Understanding and making a routine of the principles behind the action breeds success in every kind of complex and competitive pursuit. If you don't have the both the training and the mindset, you don't reach that point where you can optimize every act. Buddhists call this "spontaneous right action"; athletes call it "being in the zone." A great chef doesn't follow a recipe; she knows what will work and is willing to experiment starting with that vast base of knowledge plus the ingredients immediately at hand.

A well-executed online marketing campaign is no different. It requires the proper mindset *and* the right set of marketing skills, all customized to fit the new world of social media. A company can mimic all the right motions, but without the right philosophy, its actions are empty. A marketer who tries to keep a tight rein on every facet of an online promotion will choke it off before it can fully flower. Influencers might give your product a good review if they don't really know you, but when you build a personal relationship with them, they'll give you the benefit of the doubt if and when you stumble (and let's face it, everyone stumbles at some point).

Not long after 31 Days concluded, the copycats started to emerge. Toshiba tried a similar campaign on one of the largest technology sites around, Gizmodo.com. It generated just over 11,000 page views. The 31 Days campaign produced more than 11,000 videos, with more than 50 million page views on the 31 blogs and other sites that picked up on the program. Companies can see the mechanics of what we do at Ivy Worldwide, but no facsimile has any hope of success without the right mindset.

You can't merely mimic the moves of a judo expert and expect to become a great fighter.

The differences between a well-run and a well-mimicked campaign can be subtle. Sponsoring a paid contest on a corporate-owned, big-traffic news site such as Gizmodo removes the passion of the influencer and takes the sizzle away from the readers and what they can contribute to the project. Gizmodo (owned by Gawker Media) and Engadget (owned by AOL) focus mainly on generating traffic, so they post dozens of times a day and push down the older posts, regardless of content and importance. What results is a Twitter-like survey of what's happening now—an ever-changing survey of trending topics, often syndicated from other blogs. Don't get us wrong; we read and enjoy Gizmodo, Engadget, and similar news sites. Each serves an important function in relaying technology news and trends. Liking a site should not be the driving criterion behind choosing it for inclusion in a word-of-mouth marketing program, however. Word of mouth is about credible, transparent third-party endorsement that drives sales and conversations. Real influencers of the purchasing process dive much deeper, letting their passion show and generating the dynamic authority that spurs conversations and purchases alike. The influencers with whom we work want to post long reviews on how they use a product over time. They get the most out of the products they test, and that's precisely what their readers expect of them. In the end, influencers' readers look for a reasonable approximation of their own experience so they can avoid making bad choices that waste their time and money.

Ultimately, the placement of the Toshiba campaign made it just another online ad campaign and little more. Although it ran on a site that looked like a blog, the site was not social media as we and the vast majority of the public would define it. The campaign did not generate the interaction—the deep community conversation and participation—that generated the wave of buzz for 31 Days. Toshiba could mimic the moves, but without the right mindset, the right practice, and the right expertise, the company couldn't display a real mastery of the art of social media.

As you shift your mindset to a more judo-like philosophy, the practices and skills needed to carry out a worthy online word-of-mouth campaign become second nature. We didn't put it in these terms when we started Ivy Worldwide, but an old V.P. of ours once asked, "Where is the judo move in this?" about every idea we brought to him. That question and the parallels between our philosophy and judo's philosophy were too striking to ignore. As a result, we've shaped our approach around four pillars, each with a nod to the art and science of judo:

1) **Minimum effort and maximum efficiency** – We have talked about this a lot, but put simply, it means tapping into the network of key influencers already in place and using their existing momentum to help spread your message.

2) **Mutual benefit** – This means crafting programs that generate a strong return for the company but also provide an equally beneficial outcome for the influencers and partners with whom you work.

3) **Etiquette** – Creating personal relationships with online content producers and influencers—rather than merely trying to exploit them when you need them—is what relationships are all about.

4) **Physical education** – There must be a bridge between philosophy and practice. The judo mindset changes the ways you think about and interact with your key influencers, both on- and offline.

As we discuss each of these pillars, remember that we don't view them as rules. We have no interest in giving you a how-to checklist for the marketing mind. As judo expert Clyde Tichenor explains in his essay "The Philosophy of Judo"(available at Ohlenkamp's site, JudoInfo.com): "The U.S. Constitution and Bill of Rights are famous for what they *do not* say as well as what they *do* say. By specifying a few general rules, there is a leeway and flexibility that covers numerous unforeseen circumstances and contingencies." Consider our pillars in the same manner, as a framework for shaping how you go about designing and executing word-of-mouth marketing campaigns online.

The Art Of Minimum Effort And Maximum Efficiency

The mechanics and the art of judo are based on applying the smallest effort possible to reach the maximum performance, and that is only obtained using the suitable method, with the indispensible ability and talent.

– The Sinchijudokan Judo Institute

A commonly accepted truth in judo is that size doesn't matter. It's a generalization, of course, but the hidden skill in judo is the ability to use your opponent's momentum to your advantage. When he pulls, you push. When she pushes, you pull. A smaller fighter can throw a larger one by using his or her momentum to turn the maneuver. Take another look at the previous photo and look at how little energy the thrower is using to accomplish a rather violent maneuver.

The same concept is at play in word-of-mouth marketing, only instead of an opponent to throw, a company seeks to harness the momentum of the online community already flowing through the Internet. It is only a fight if you try to do everything yourself while wasting a lot of energy (read: money and time). Instead, go with the flow and you'll get further, faster. The most successful word-of-mouth marketing campaigns emerge when companies engage the expertise, audiences, and enthusiasm of its key influencers. We saw it work to perfection during 31 Days of the Dragon's contests to give away 31 of HP's flagship notebooks. But it works just as well—and sometimes even better—without the freebies and without a top-of-the-line product.

In March 2009, well after 31 Days, HP came back to us with one of the toughest challenges we've seen to date. The company planned to launch a promotion for its Pavilion dv2 notebook in early April, with the idea that it could settle in as a mainstay PC for the back-to-school shopping season later in the year. The product was by no means a dog, but it wasn't exactly the Dragon, either. Making things more difficult, it was packaged running Windows Vista—despite the fact that Microsoft already had announced the pending release of Vista's much-ballyhooed successor, Windows 7. Nor would the dv2 run on the newer, faster, more power-efficient Intel processors, also set to launch later in the year; instead, it ran a value-oriented AMD processor. To top it off, we had to generate buzz during a back-to-school season dominated by Apple, specifically targeting the college-aged crowd. We regularly lecture at the University of Texas and the University of Washington and know that there, as at most colleges, roughly 75% of the students use, buy and love Apple notebooks.

We knew the dv2 wouldn't blow anyone away on its merits alone, but we also knew it could do just about anything most college students would want to do with their laptops. Students could use the dv2 on productive schoolwork during the day, and then turn it into an entertainment center at night. A cynic might not have called then dv2 "hip," but the laptop had a certain style, plus it was light and easily portable. We realized we had to present it in a way that showed all the things a college student could do with it, so we figured, why not have the dv2 provide the entertainment for a party? And lo, the "party-in-a-box" concept was born.

We approached some of the top college bloggers we knew and suggested that they throw parties—on HP's dime—promoting their sites. We wanted to provide them a way to elevate their brands above and beyond their online peers and rivals, but more than that, we wanted them to put on great parties for people just like them. And yeah, we asked them to work the product into the parties in subtle, welcoming fashions. Don't make it all about the product, we told them, make the product complementary to the experience you want to provide in the first place. In essence, use the dv2 to provide the entertainment for your event—and thus make it a conversation piece for the partygoers.

From that seed of an idea, we released the idea back into the proverbial wild, and the college bloggers took off with it. They came up with the catchy names for their event dates concurrent with other goings-on important to students, agendas for catering and entertainment—everything. And then they promoted the hell out of the parties on their sites, Facebook pages, Twitter feeds, and every other means of online communication at their disposal. This was their chance to be big men on campus, and they weren't about to let it pass. The crew at Festival-Crashers.com, who follow all the major outdoor music festivals, decided to throw an after-party following the Lollapalooza Tour's stop in Chicago. CollegeCandy.com put on a Cosmo-esque party in New York City. And the guys behind HackCollege.com threw a soiree near the UCLA campus, complete with shuttle services at the end of the night.

One party had cocktails named after the sponsoring site and the dv2. The HackCollege party used the dv2 as a virtual jukebox for songs and video, which was displayed on flat-panel screens throughout the venue. All the sites ran the night's entertainment through the dv2 notebook we wanted to promote. We might never have thought of that, but we sure recognized the idea's brilliance when we heard it. This was experiential marketing at its finest. Better yet, the parties cost HP about $4,000 each and garnered more than several hundred attendees each in person and tens of thousands more online. It didn't cost the influencers a penny. The influencers didn't have to charge their guests a cent, either. All we asked of the influencers was that they showcase the dv2 in a way that they and their readers would appreciate, and in the process generate some content—for their sites and for HP—chronicling all the fun and showing how the dv2 naturally fit into the lives of college students.

The HackCollege.com Summer Jam Session worked like a charm for Kelly Sutton and Chris Lesinski, the guys behind HackCollege.com and the party in Los Angeles. They took photos during their event and invited people to the site to tag themselves and comment on the party. "We had people standing in line at a bar to use a laptop," Sutton said. "It was pretty remarkable. It was like an Apple store, except with free booze and people dancing. For a company like HP, with their market share among students and image being eaten away by Apple, that's the best they can hope for. And they were willing to go out on a limb and experiment and do things that haven't been done before."

We never could have generated that sort of buzz among college students on our own. Post-event search-engine ranking for the dv2 far surpassed the corporate microsite built to promote the notebook, and conversation about the device began to rival the buzz about more expensive offerings from Apple. HP might have been able to piece that together, but it would've cost a hell of a lot more than they spent on design and execution of all the events.

And the results speak for themselves:

- 20% average increase in sales volume over comparable markets (33% in peak markets)
- More than 4000 attendees at all events
- More than 10,000 contest entrants
- More than 5 million monthly visitors to the combined sites
- More than 24,000 Twitter followers added during the campaign

- More than 8,000 Facebook friends added during the campaign
- 1,675 photos uploaded by the influencers during the campaign
- 125 blog posts created by the influencers and other bloggers picking up the campaign
- More than 80 other sites propagated HP events and content around HP's Envy brand

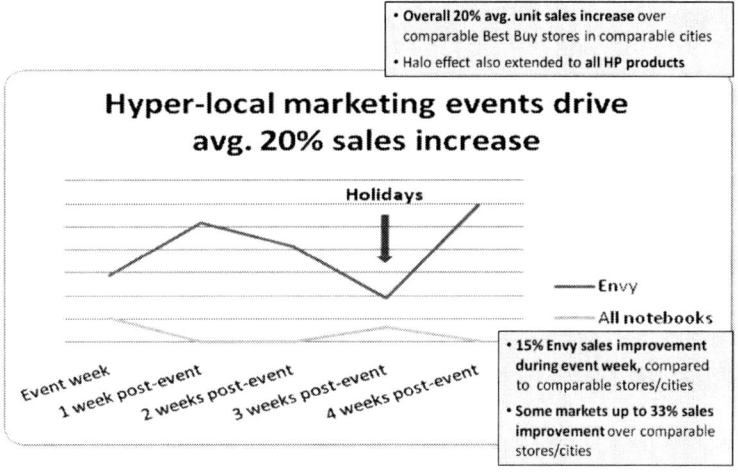

Chart showing sales gains provided by our Envy Party-in-a-Box campaign. [4]
Photo from: http://vkoreanmartialarts.com.

This is the art of minimum effort and maximum efficiency. We could list just about every one of our marketing campaigns as an example of this, and we could provide dozens of reasons that such an approach helps companies reach a broader audience with a better message and less effort, but two reasons for its success stand out:

[4] Sales improvement determined by comparing against control stores in similarly sized markets with similar market share. Sales volume improvement calculated from baseline unit sales comprising 4 weeks prior to campaign, normalized against comparable periodic seasonality.

1) This approach allows a company to reach an increasingly diverse and diffuse audience
2) The approach gives customers a chance to lend authority to a message by putting it into their own words

Reaching A Diverse Audience

A lot of small things had to come together to make what we call "party in a box" successful, but the fact that these college bloggers took it over was what made it such a success—for both themselves and HP. By putting the project in the bloggers' hands and ceding control of the project—and yet ensuring that their output aligned with HP's business objectives—we found a way to credibly and transparently reach a rather hard-to-reach and -engage audience with a low-end notebook. College students offer an attractive demographic for a host of consumer-products companies, but they can be notoriously difficult to engage with any authenticity. Working with these key influencers, we could ride their momentum as they spread the word about their parties and, by extension, HP's computer.

Every marketer struggles to figure out how to position a product to meet an individual customer's needs. How do I craft a campaign that reaches a wide range of people and yet touches each of them on an individual level? It's no easy task, but social media has provided powerful new tools for mass customization. In particular, blogs have helped close the gap between the masses and the individual. By working cooperatively and collaboratively with bloggers, a company can craft one message that the bloggers tailor to their respective audiences, thus making it their own. In essence, the company produces its overarching message, and by allowing each of the bloggers to present the message in their own individual ways, they allow the influencers to customize the message for their audiences (without really even realizing it).

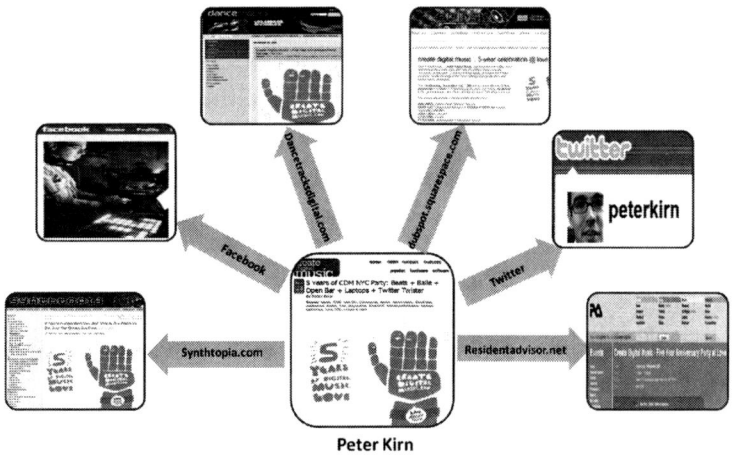

Peter Kirn
CreateDigitalMusic.com

Influential bloggers are consummate marketers and self-promoters, utilizing every available avenue to raise awareness. In addition to being presented in posts on his own blog, news of the Peter Kirn and CreateDigitalMusic.com event was re-posted to more than 25 other blogs and sites as well as re-tweeted by many of his numerous followers.

"There's no way of corralling 100 college blogs. There's no way of really doing that. There's no program to do that for you. There's no network of blogs or campus reps," said Lesinski, the cofounder of HackCollege.com. "It takes a different kind of effort to reach out to an individual student at 100 different campuses across the nation. That's different from giving money to an ad buyer and saying, 'Buy me ads.' It takes an entirely different attitude and approach, and it takes giving someone else a lot of autonomy."

Letting The Customer Reshape The Message

Giving up autonomy can strike the fear in the hearts of most marketers, who remain bound to the traditional mindset and approach. To be fair, that's understandable. When a company puts its message into the hands of its key influencers and enthusiasts, it faces the very real likelihood that the messages will transform into something else. When done properly, however, that transformation is an opportunity, not a risk. For a bad product or a company that ignores its customers—a business that doesn't earn the right to have customers tell its story, as noted marketing author Jeanne Bliss puts it—this undoubtedly is a risk, and a significant one at that. What's more, even for some of the best companies, it can backfire.

Our good friend Gary Spangler is the e-business leader for DuPont's electronic and communication technologies group and a board member at WOMMA. Spangler knows online word-of-mouth marketing as well as anyone at a Fortune 500 company does. Not long after 31 Days had concluded, he decided to try a similar campaign with some of DuPont's key online influencers. The campaign never got off the ground. The main reason for this boiled down to DuPont trying to retain too much control of the program, running the campaign and giveaway entirely by themselves. That tied up the program in DuPont's legal group, removing all the bloggers' flexibility and thus their reason for even participating. Needless to say, once the lawyers got out the red pens and the bloggers' hands were tied, the campaign was grounded before it even got to the launch pad.

Programs of this sort work only if you stay out of the way. Set up the when and where, but leave everything else to the bloggers. When a company does that—assuming a decent product and a good relationship with its influencers (more on that later)—this approach can lead to incredible opportunities. Influencers will take the message and transform it. They'll put your message into their own words, giving it that boost of dynamic authority and customizing it for their audiences. What's more, they add their own endorsement to it (again, pre-suming the product is worthy of endorsement), which is something no company can replicate, even with bottomless resources. In fact, the influencers might even go so far as to defend you from your critics when these go on the attack.

It comes down to a simple new truth in the Internet age: Your customers own a piece of your brand now. This has been established ad nauseam by other social media and Web 2.0 pundits, but it's worth emphasizing yet again. If someone can post professional-quality content about your product, that's brand ownership. That was impossible 10 years ago, but today almost anyone can do it, and they can beam it out worldwide and instantaneously. As a result, it's imperative that companies shed their fear of the Web's unknowns, grapple with this new reality, and find a way to use it to their advantage. They have to wade into the fray and begin collaborating with their key influencers, tapping into the momentum of these self-designated brand envoys, and use it to turbo-charge their own messaging, communications, sales, support, and every other aspect of the marketing discipline.

With a minimum of effort, a company can achieve maximum results. We've said it before. Marketing online is like a rip current in the ocean. Try to swim directly back to shore, and you'll quickly tire and might even drown, but swim *with* the current while making your way toward land and you'll make it back. You can't overpower it; instead, go with the flow. Without the help of your key influencers, enthusiasts, and evangelists, your best-laid plans will go nowhere—á la the Visa campaign.

Mutual Satisfaction

The practice of judo must bring joy and satisfaction, interaction with companions, the study and investigation of forms, collaboration and mutual development. ... Judo has to be constituted as an effective art with mutual satisfaction.

– Sinchijudokan Judo Institute

Anyone who's had the dubious pleasure of attending a trade show knows how lame the corporate party can be, so when we started planning Party-in-a-Box for HP, we made damn sure it didn't turn into a corporate launch party. (Hell, we had to make sure it didn't turn into one of our own parties.) These events were targeted at college students, and as much as we'd like to think we're hip on today's college scene, we don't party like that anymore (not for lack of trying—it's just that we *can't*). HP, to its credit, understood this entirely, so we turned over much of the planning to the bloggers and let them come up with events that their audiences would enjoy.

"What surprised me was there was a company out there willing to actually give some responsibility to these college bloggers out there," said HackCollege.com's Kelly Sutton. "Sure, we didn't get too much of a traffic increase from the event, but it was another nice thing to do for our readers and they thoroughly enjoyed themselves, so it was an easy decision. It's not just another blog post, it was an extension of our brand. We bridged the gap from an online presence to the real-world and that really helped secure our image as innovators. The new format and extensive interaction was the key to all of it."

Robert Bardunias from CollegeCandy.com also saw the benefit. "When we first found out about the possibility to throw a party for our readers while co-marketing the HP dv2 notebook, we absolutely jumped at the opportunity. The notebook was a perfect fit for our readers, and for the first time, our editors had a chance to meet in person with their loyal audience while giving back to them at the same time. The dv2 Party-in-a-Box campaign was a phenomenal success for us, providing an exciting occasion to bring the CollegeCandy.com brand to life."

Bloggers and other content producers want nothing more than to deliver the goods for their audience. If they don't provide engaging content and an engrossing experience, a dynamic discussion or an occasional giveaway, they don't draw new followers—or worse, they run the risk of losing the ones they already have. For those who rely on their sites for income, readership equals money, so a company that approaches them with something that does nothing to engage and build their audiences will lose the bloggers' interest pretty quickly. Conversely, companies that present bloggers with ideas that can generate more traffic or raise a site's profile will be met with a warm embrace by the bloggers, and those bloggers will go out of their way to improve on the idea to ensure that *it works*—for both audience and company alike.

Still, different influencers need different things. The technology bloggers with whom we often work tend to be geeks at heart. For example, an interview with the CEO of a big company might not interest their audience. Instead, for most bloggers and their readers, the sexy interview is the one with the engineers and product designers. They love the ins and outs of how a company pieces together a product and why the company chooses to add this or that feature. They love hearing what the engineers and designers think about new technology and product trends coming down the line. In essence, they want to feel like insiders with a glimpse—as much as a company can provide—of what's happening and what's coming up. Given the chance, influencers will provide feedback and insight to help improve products in development. And what's more, they'll actively—even relentlessly—market any product that includes the ideas, innovations, and suggestions they've provided. This is the essence of what we call "customer co-marketing."

The same approach might not work for a different group of influencers, however. Some might actually prefer the exclusive CEO interview. Some might just want to share an experience that few people ever get to have by getting closer to a company than the average bear. The U.S. Navy, of all organizations, did a tremendous job of co-marketing when it brought 15 of the Internet's most popular bloggers onboard the aircraft carrier *USS Nimitz* in May 2009. (Frankly, if the military can find a way to do this in spite of its rampant bureaucracy and need for secrecy, your company can do it, too.) The Navy gave bloggers like Beth Blecherman and Robert Scoble, and, on a separate trip, our friend Chris Pirillo, virtually unfettered access to the ship and its crew, keeping little other than the most sensitive military areas off limits. The crew gave extensive facility tours and explanations of the ship's operations. The Navy even strapped the bloggers into a jet so they could feel the sheer power and adrenaline rush of a carrier takeoff and landing. The Navy brings civilians aboard on a regular basis, but it had never invited a group that could generate the word-of-mouth buzz these bloggers could. And did the Navy *ever* benefit from the "risk"—just use your favorite search engine to have a look at the sheer quantity and mainly positive quality of the bloggers' stories about their experiences.

Unfortunately, we usually see examples of organizations either absolutely botching or just completely overlooking opportunities to engage their key influencers. We've worked with HP extensively, but they're not immune to the occasional mistake. James Kendrick, the "JK" behind the popular tech blog JKontherun.com, lives near Houston and just blocks away from HP's sprawling campus there. Kendrick writes a blog focused on mobile technology and notebook computers. He had a half million readers in 2007—most of them favorably inclined toward HP products—yet the company had not invited him to visit an office he could've walked to in 5 minutes. We eventually found out about this and rectified the situation, making sure to get him invited—and HP has invited him back dozens of times since, having gotten into the habit of giving him a steady stream of information for his site. Like we always say, if a blogger is working closely with you and is consistently discussing your products, it creates less space for him or her to spend ink on the competition.

This isn't rocket science. Give your key influencers content that helps them build their audiences, and they'll be all the more likely to use it in ways that benefit you. The idea of giving information out to the "Big Bad Blogosphere" plainly scares the hell out of marketers stuck in the traditional mindset, however; the mere notion of releasing unscripted information into the wild is what scares them. The possibility that every message won't be treated as a Matisse masterpiece challenges their professional bearing and self-conception, and let's be honest: this attitude is rooted in a lack of true understanding of this critical audience combined with an avoidance of change. We're all guilty of this tendency at one time or another, but recognizing the issue is the first step toward correcting the problem (kudos to you for reading this far!). Nevertheless, it's easy to design and execute a marketing strategy that provides as much benefit for influencers as it does for your company. The hard part is abandoning the traditional mindset enough to let yourself actually go out and *do it*. A whole new approach to marketing opens up with recognizing that the old rules no longer apply and making this simple shift in philosophy.

Going into 31 Days, we were scared to death of what influencers might think of the idea. It was, after all, a *huge* project in the early days of our company. But we knew on a fundamental level that for any marketing project to succeed, we had to make full use of the power of social media by tapping into the influencers' momentum. In other words, we knew we had to achieve the greatest efficiency with the minimum effort. And we knew that the only way to do that was to make sure the influencers with whom we collaborated got their piece of the pie, too.

We had to make sure the 31 influencers got as much or more out of the campaign as HP did. So what did we do to get started? We called the influencers up and asked their advice. We laid out the idea and solicited their feedback about to how to improve it. We didn't get a single suggestion in that sense, just praise—not because the bloggers didn't care, but because from the start we'd designed 31 Days with their welfare in mind. If you craft a terrible program, people will complain about it from the start, even if you give them a role in developing it. But because our starting point puts the influencers first, we've never run into that problem. With the right mindset, neither will you.

This is not to say we do not consider our clients' needs or objectives, or that we subordinate their needs and objectives to those of the influencers. Instead, we endeavor to find the intersection of both, which has to exist, given the influencers' interest in the company and its products.

A Little Fertilizer For Branching Out

Jason Dunn owns Thoughts Media Inc., a company based in Calgary, Canada, that includes a number of blogs he oversees and to which he contributes. When we think of tech bloggers, Dunn is on our short list. He didn't have the massive audience of some other more popular blogs at the time of the 31 Days campaign, but for us it was a no-brainer to bring him in. Dunn had started a new YouTube channel and wanted a way to drive more traffic to it. Because we left the details of the giveaway to each blogger, he realized he could use 31 Days to help build his nascent YouTube presence. He cross-promoted his blog with the new video channel, and traffic to both ballooned. By the end of the month, according to him, he had thousands of subscribers on YouTube and about 1,200 comments posted to the videos on his new channel.

Dunn said he would've jumped at a chance to participate in 31 Days even if HP had made the requirements for participation too restrictive to be of use in establishing himself on YouTube. "I'm always interested in things that benefit my community, like giving away a product," he said, "but using this as a mechanism to build up my own profile makes it more appealing. There's a double-benefit. My readers can win a prize, and I can build out my brand's online presence. I understand the core of why HP did this: They're a public company, and they're about selling products. But by giving us the flexibility to utilize 31 Days as a tool to promote our own Web properties in the process was unselfish in a way that wouldn't detract from what HP was trying to do."

That's what we mean by mutual satisfaction. If you set up a campaign with the *when* and the *where*, then leave everything else to your influencers, it will work. Like Dunn, Chris Pirillo used 31 Days to strengthen his YouTube channel. Xavier Lanier, owner of the popular Notebooks.com family of blogs, established a collection of reader forums with the help of the 31 Days traffic. Many of the bloggers, like Dunn and Lanier, already had plans; the campaign merely allowed them to jumpstart their ideas.

Etiquette

Judo has certain formalities and protocols in its practice. They come from tradition, from a community of wise people who make those values the nucleus of its existence. The customs in judo are based on mutual respect, simplicity, deference, service and courtesy.

— Sinchijudokan Judo Institute

The Party-in-a-Box campaign tapped into the momentum of a few key influencers to generate sales from a hard-to-reach audience (read: achieving minimum effort with maximum efficiency). Along with 31 Days, Party-in-a-Box also illustrated the willingness of those same influencers to help your cause if you provide them something of benefit to them in return (mutual satisfaction). None of that would've happened, however, if we hadn't made a point of building personal relationships with all the bloggers in our "virtual Rolodex." Case in point: The HP partnership with the NBA almost killed Party-in-a-Box before it could get off the ground, and it took skilled intervention on the part of the influencers—brokered by Ivy Worldwide's relationships with each of them—to avoid that unhappy outcome.

In support of its launch of the Pavilion dv2 notebook, HP had crafted a multiphase marketing campaign that took into account its partnership with Microsoft. It also included a joint promotion with the National Basketball Association. The first phase of the program was expected to drive Web traffic to an HP microsite where visitors could enter a sweepstakes for NBA playoff tickets. Simply put, it didn't work. When traffic only trickled into the microsite, HP called on Ivy Worldwide to help boost traffic. We did so with great reluctance, because our experience told us that microsites rarely work. When they do work, it's because they're backed by a big marketing spend, not any inherently viral aspect of the site itself—and the success lasts only as long as the company keeps the spending in place. In short, the situation was like most of those we come across:

This one aspect of the HP dv2 launch was based more on driving gratification for the brand than on driving something truly meaningful, such as sales.

A job is a job, however, and we went to our bloggers to pitch a somewhat unusual juxtaposition of brands, asking them to link to the HP–NBA microsite and improve its traffic draw. The only measure of success stipulated by HP was the number of people visiting that site, which in any event was scheduled to go away at the end of the month. The site would offer zero long-term value to the influencers, and they, of course, realized that immediately. We had to call in some favors to get them to sign onto the microsite phase of the dv2 launch, and for that we had to trust in and lean on the personal relationships we'd forged with dozens of online content producers over the past several years.

"We get a lot of unsolicited emails," said Sutton, the Hack-College.com cofounder. "We read all of them, but we don't read all of each one. It's pretty easy to tell who wants to develop a relationship and who wants to just push their product. The fact that Ivy went through enough trouble to figure out our names, read our sites and explain the campaign in their first email definitely made them stick out." Think about that: We went online and learned their names. We explained to them what we hoped to accomplish. And, most important, we outlined what was in it for them if they joined forces with us. This isn't exactly solving the secrets of the universe. In fact, it's little more than common courtesy. Simply getting to know your key influencers can unlock all kinds of possibilities for your entire range of marketing activities. They'll provide honest feedback on products and the marketing efforts behind them. They'll give you the benefit of the doubt when you screw something up (and we *all* screw up at one point or another), often going to great lengths to defend you from your harshest critics. They'll help spread your message to their audiences and, assuming you've identified the right influencers to work with from the outset, will portray your product (in a usually positive light) to more potential customers than you probably realize.

"What Ivy Worldwide has done, it doesn't seem like it should be that special," said Dunn. "It's not like they've unlocked some molecular secret. It's common sense: You talk to people. You engage them. You give them the flexibility to differentiate themselves from their peers, and you just let them go with it. It's pretty much common sense, but common sense isn't all that common when you're talking about large corporations." In fact, most companies and PR agencies fail miserably at building relationships with online influencers. Most marketing departments just avoid the whole process altogether, because building relationships with key influencers takes work and offers no guarantees. It certainly doesn't mean those influencers will hop right into your corporate hip pocket. We cannot tell you how many times a PR agency or in-house person swears they know the "bloggers" when, in reality, they simply do not. When they say "know," that's usually PR-speak for "I have an email address … I think." We have seen many bloggers politely correct PR people by saying, "I don't think we have met," or "I don't remember that, but it's nice to meet you."

Etiquette has to be obvious. The instant a blogger's audience gets a sniff of a sellout, they're gone—and the bloggers know this better than anyone. Like the bushido, the code of honor for judo and other Japanese martial arts, the rules of what we'll call etiquette still apply. Company interactions with bloggers must remain transparent and honest, and bloggers must maintain the same standards with their audience. None of this means that interactions will always be nice. Your friend will tell you when you have spinach stuck between your teeth, or when that dress really *does* make your butt look big, or when you have a giant zit on your forehead. They'll tell you your baby is ugly. What you may not realize is that most bloggers won't go about yelling, "Ha! Look at my friend's ugly kid!" If they respect who you are and how much you value your relationship with them, they'll keep that between you and them, allowing you to do something about your "issues" outside the public eye. This is merely mutual respect at work, just like in any other well-founded relationship in the adult world.

The Cocktail Party

We approach relationships with influencers like we'd approach a cocktail party. We've all met the guy at the business happy hour who wants nothing more than to drone on about himself. No one wants to be subjected to that, and almost everyone moves on to more interesting conversations with others in the room.

The same rules apply to the blogosphere as well. It's a conversation, a dialogue, not one-way transmissions. Talking points kill the conversation at a cocktail party, and they kill conversation in the blogosphere. If you go into a monologue or come across as wanting to talk about only yourself, people suddenly need to head to the bar or to the bathroom or exclaim, "Whew, just look how late it's getting!" In the world of social media, marketers have to be social as well. They need to set up and build real relationships with their company's key influencers. When we go to conferences, it feels like a reunion between Ivy Worldwide and the influencers we've been working with for ages. We catch up with each other. We give each other a good ribbing, all in fun. We ask about each other's families. We laugh and joke for a bit. We enjoy hanging out with these friends, and, yes, we get down to business eventually. But we attend to the relationships first. The world of social media is social, both online and in person.

Rob Bushway ran a popular blog called GottaBeMobile.com. He recently sold it to Xavier Lanier, who added it to his collection of blogs under the Notebooks.com umbrella. Bushway has a lot of clout with highly mobile people who use laptops, tablet PCs, and other portable computers. We worked with him on several projects over the years and got to know him very well, so when we heard that his daughter's ongoing illness had taken a turn for the worse, we had no choice but to try to do something for him. Bushway and his family were away from home at the time of the unfortunate turn in circumstances, in another state, and, of course, could use a hand from friends. What did we do? We arranged with other blogger friends to pool money to cover airfare and hotel costs for one of Bushway's friends, who came to help manage the situation, look after the kids and generally take up the slack in a moment of crisis. "I don't recall ever being treated that way by any agency," Bushway said. "These guys believe in relationships. They volunteered to do what they did. I don't mind that being published. That's meant more to me than any type of giveaway or promotion they've put on for my readers. That's why I'm here on the phone."

We didn't decide to tell this story to make you think we're saints. We added this anecdote because it shows how serious we are when we talk about developing real, personal relationships with content producers and key influencers. For us, it was the right thing to do and there was no question about doing it. Companies eventually will have to learn this and empower their own people to connect with and build real, live, give-and-take relationships with the people who can help them reach their customers. It's not easy to do, especially for a company used to pulling all the strings, but once you start, it gets easier.

When we first started our firm, back when we still called ourselves Buzz Corps, we put a simple message on the back of our business cards, encouraging people to do a Web search of our names to find out more about what others said about us—after all, we didn't expect a potential client to simply take *our* word for it. Similarly, when we contact a blogger for the first time, we encourage him or her to talk to their peers about us. We do this in part because we're very confident in what will be said about us, and also because we know they'll do it anyway. We want every new person we meet to understand that we're not looking to negotiate another angle that will benefit only our clients. We don't want them to fear that we'll merely go through our clients' talking points, leaving them to sort out what it all means for their readers. Instead, we want them to know that we're the guys and gals they'll actually *want* to hang out with at a cocktail party, because we'll actually get to know them. And once we know each other and are comfortable, if it happens to suit both of us, we'll talk business. Later.

Change The Rules

Let's state what's already obvious to anyone who's not a marketer or professional PR hack: Marketing and public relations in corporate America come with way too many restrictions. Clearly, certain legal and corporate regulations are a good thing. They protect trade secrets, limit insider trading, and lessen the chances for a troubling conflict of interest. We're supportive of those sorts of controls. And when it comes to marketing through social media, we wholeheartedly support the *de facto* rules there, too: Be transparent; disclose any potential conflicts of interest; be honest with the company, influencer, and audience. We didn't leave our prior jobs to get away from rules; we left to get away from the mindset so deeply embedded in corporate America that every interaction had to be some sort of transaction.

We left behind the corporate guide for dealing with journalists, bloggers, and other content producers and chose instead to let a basic sense of friendship be the first and best guide to our interactions. If we lie or do something unethical, we'll jeopardize our friendships. When we develop real relationships with people and get to know them apart from the work they do, we're working under the set of rules associated with any friendship. Sometimes we're in a position of power, sometimes they are. Either way, if you help them when you can, they'll do the same for you.

Unfortunately, when most marketing and PR professionals put on their business hats, every situation becomes a negotiation. That's the worst way to work with online content producers. If you call your key influencers only when you need them, they might still listen to what you have to say, but if you develop real friendships with them—if you go to them with something in hand (even if it's only a desire to really get to know them) instead of with your hand out—they'll provide so much more. They'll offer feedback on products in your development pipeline. They'll connect you with their audiences in ways you can't manage on your own. They'll publicly endorse what's good about your products. They'll talk to you first when something isn't right. And when your company comes under unwarranted criticism, they'll take to your defense.

They'll give you the benefit of the doubt, as true friends would.

Physical Education

A positive, fast mind is necessary and needs to remain open and disciplined. In addition, one must have a dynamic, organized, perfected, generous, humble and loving spirit of the natural thing; and a mature control of the emotions that allows one to act with suitable temperament and character.

— Sinchijudokan Judo Institute

When judo experts talk about the highest orders of competition, they don't talk about reflexes, strength, and stamina; they talk about a hyper-alert, agile mind and an iron will. The top judo masters have no doubts. Novices pause to think about the next move, and in that instant, the window for successful action closes. The expert judo mind doesn't worry about quick reactions and silly ploys to set up a talented opponent, judo expert Ohlenkamp says. At the highest levels of judo competition, participants make only the slightest of mistakes and give their opponents very few opportunities to exploit them. A winning participant not only senses his or her opponent's next move but anticipates the exact moment when it will occur. As Ohlenkamp explains it, "You know it from the feel of a situation you've felt before." It becomes an innate understanding that can come only through years of practice and study. It becomes second nature.

Fortunately for us, and despite the speed with which the world works today, marketers don't have to react quite as quickly as judo masters. Even so, marketing has its own consequences for laggards. The most successful marketers share an innate understanding of how to reach their customers and can act quickly when haste is required. They develop a keen feel for the best ways to engage customers and compel those customers to buy. They don't have a magical sixth sense, any more than a top judo fighter does; they've simply worked and studied long enough to "know it from the feel of a situation they've felt before."

INo matter how much experience you have, it still takes constant vigilance and practice to recognize the opportunities in a constantly shifting social media ecosystem. Today, marketers must adapt, as the judo expert would when a top-flight opponent does something new and unexpected. In a certain sense, we at Ivy Worldwide got lucky because the rise of social media played right into the style of marketing we already employed and believed in, but we also worked our tails off—and still do—to constantly improve our mindset and hone our word-of-mouth marketing skills. Working with content producers comes as second nature to us, but we cannot take it for granted. We still learn from every interaction with an influencer or client. We get better with every new campaign we design and execute. We pore through our most successful campaigns to understand the errors as well as the keys to success.

We could've walked away from that fateful Windows Vista campaign thinking we'd managed to pull off a coup, but we couldn't escape the fact that in some senses we'd also dodged a bullet. And being compulsive marketers, we had to know *exactly* why and where the errors had been made. Far too many companies want to take the most mediocre results and put a positive spin on them. We hear people crow, "We got our product mentioned on Twitter," or "We got someone to post about the latest release!" and watch as they check it off their list of quarterly goals. But nowadays, when virtually every company has some sort of social-media presence (as ham-fisted as many of them are), only the well-executed programs will differentiate your company from its rivals. Marketers no longer have the option to claim credit solely for "doing social media" because customers, the blogosphere, and critics will no longer give you credit solely for merely showing up. Those days are gone. You have to do it right, as of today, and the only way to do it right is to constantly learn and adapt as things change—and then do it over, and over, and over again, each time better than the last.

The soaring use of social media has changed the entire marketing landscape, but it has changed most radically the way consumers generate and spread that coveted word-of-mouth buzz. Instead of marketing *at* a target audience, the new breed of successful companies now must master the art of customer co-marketing—marketing *with* their audience. This cross-functional, interdisciplinary approach cultivates a customer's total involvement with your brand. It develops mutually beneficial relationships and campaigns that allow buyers to become partners with you in most everything they do.

By engaging in customer co-marketing, you empower your best customers to help identify, design, and support your products. You let them deliver your messages to the market with an authenticity and credibility your company can't generate on its own. And you can do all this at a fraction of the cost of traditional methods.

This shift has trapped a lot of great marketing experts in recent years. We've seen it catch some of the best—people who could craft killer campaigns for traditional media but who are now struggling to grasp the reality of social media and the changes it has wrought on customer expectations. The rise of social media has fundamentally changed the traditional business-customer, marketer-audience relationships. Cooperation now has replaced negotiation as the underlying mindset for those interactions. Fail to understand that fundamental change, and all your past years of work and study won't help you in the future. This is your new reality as a marketer, whether you realize it—and like it—or not.

An Art And A Science

Anything worth doing has both a philosophical and practical side. So far, we've spent a lot of time talking about the philosophical aspects of word-of-mouth marketing. We make no apologies for that. The practical skills needed for a successful marketing campaign look quite similar, whether used in traditional media or on blogs, YouTube, and Facebook, yet when looked at from this new mindset—when traditional marketers adopt a *social* philosophy and don't merely slap their current practices onto a new medium—the skills that once looked so similar now appear strikingly different.

At Ivy Worldwide, we've applied the judo allegory to marketing via social media because aside from being an apt one, it also perfectly portrays the necessary balance between mind and body—or between philosophy and practice. To be black-belt caliber, you have to internalize the discipline of both mind and body. And until you internalize it, you cannot excel at it. If you rely on rote, mechanical execution of judo moves without understanding why they work and how they work, you'll get suboptimal results at best and, more likely, outright failure.

The same is true for word-of-mouth marketing campaigns: You have to internalize the mindset. The fundamental change toward marketing from a social mindset then shifts everything erected atop that foundation. We can't stress this enough: What we do is both art and science. The philosophical aspect will mean nothing to your bottom line without the practical. As a result, the two are inseparable, just as the philosophy and the physical skills of judo are inseparable. We'll keep returning to a social mindset, but we also need to address the practical side of social media marketing—the five steps to mastering social-media judo.

1) *Ukemi,* **or learning to fall** – Mistakes are inevitable; problems will arise. The company that handles them with aplomb has the opportunity to enhance its reputation.

2) ***Uchikomi*, or mastering the basics** – Many traditional marketing skills come into play in social media, but most companies stumble when putting them into play. Integrating social media throughout the company can amplify all the other marketing tools.

3) ***Kuzushi*, or focus on balance** – Companies have to go with the flow, but knowing when and where to jump into the fray will save time, energy, and resources while keeping the message intact.

4) ***Randori*, or free practice** – Social media marketing does not exist in a vacuum. Companies must integrate social media into a more holistic, multichannel marketing campaign.

5) ***Shiai*, or the contest** – The point of it all. In judo, the objective is to win the match, and in business and marketing, your job is to grow the bottom line.

To help guide you through each step, we take a consistent approach to each of the five chapters. We'll start with an explanation of each step and how you can put it into practice, but that doesn't mean much without the real-life examples that prove the point—through both successes and failures. The best judo experts learn as much from throwing as they do from getting thrown. Marketers must do the same.

CHAPTER 3

Ukemi:
Learning To Fall

ANY SERIOUS JUDO STUDENT GETS slammed to the mat regularly. It comes with the territory. In practice or in competition, the youngest or the most advanced student—everyone who practices judo—gets ample opportunity to play the *uke*, the thrown fighter. Almost by necessity, the earliest lessons for all judo students focus on how to fall properly. Without that training, injuries are bound to occur.

Safety underlies every falling exercise, but the training's true benefits extend well beyond the physical skills. By teaching how a throw feels, the practice imparts an essential knowledge of more advanced judo techniques. It instills confidence and understanding in students, who, with it, can then fight more boldly without a fear of injury holding them back. As Ohlenkamp explains, "Unless one understands the correct positioning of *uke* (the one receiving the throw), it is difficult to fully master the action of *tori* (the thrower)." A fighter who does not know how to fall typically will worry too much about defense, limiting the bold and aggressive actions necessary to overcome a foe and win the match.

Ukemi focuses on receiving a fall gracefully so a person can rise up and continue the struggle. An attentive student sees the fall as a lesson rather than a defeat. She does not dwell on it or get upset by a fall. She does not fear the fall, thus freeing herself to take risks and lending a certain deliberateness to her actions. A student tries to avoid the throw, of course, and she understands the dangers of falling, but fear of a fall by no means paralyzes the fighter into inaction. "Learning to fall frees us to take risks and show more courage and commitment in our actions," Ohlenkamp says. "It allows us to remain in control of our future and not give in to unfortunate circumstances."

Fear of social media has crippled most companies. In fact, it still cripples far too many to the point of incapacitation. They hear the horror stories, without realizing that almost all mistakes stem from a company's own incompetence, lack of planning, and poor understanding of the medium itself. As we've stated before, failure has little to do with the risks inherent to social media. In other words, all marketing involves risks of one sort or another.

Some companies are convinced that bloggers want nothing more than to take down corporate America, but for 99% of bloggers, nothing of the sort is true. In their fear, companies move in the opposite direction at the exact moment they should be taking decisive advantage of their rivals, who themselves doubtless share similar fears. Rather than take advantage of a massive opportunity to work with influential voices who better reach the companies' customers, most companies instead take a command-and-control approach to social media or just avoid it altogether. They take the path of least resistance. It is human nature and quite reasonable, really: They're afraid to fall. They're afraid to fail, and that fear has paralyzed them.

We've spent years studying the mistakes and successes of social-media marketing campaigns, both ours and others'. We've discovered a stubborn truth: Sometimes the best efforts will fail, and sometimes a middling product can produce spectacular results. A marketing professional needs not only the courage to try new things but also the discipline to study the failures and successes alike—to know why something works or doesn't. That's especially true when it comes to social media. The space is still young enough that experiments will work, sometimes for all the wrong reasons. As the ecosystem matures and its bones start to harden, room for experimentation will remain, but the limits on what works and what doesn't will only get tighter. A program you call a success in today's adolescent social-media space might generate similar results five years from now but be deemed an epic failure because your competitor found a way to do the same thing better, faster, and for less money.

Marketers who approach social media with courage and discipline not only learn to avoid past mistakes (their own and others') but also continually gain confidence in new methods for the future. Like a judo masters who don't worry about falling, they no longer feel bound by a nagging fear of potential failure. They make fewer mistakes, but when they do slip up, they handle it gracefully and quickly learn from their errors. We can't promise everything will come up roses for every marketing campaign. The social-media environment is still chaotic and immature, and that's not going to change any time soon. Adopting the right mindset will help you draw allies, though, and it will help moderate your mistakes and maximize the potential of your efforts. If you have the maturity to recognize and embrace the mistakes that do occur, learning from the criticism that inevitably arises and adapting when campaigns take on lives of their own, you will feel freer to try bolder ideas— ideas that your competitors will have to spend months or years trying to copy.

The Graceful Fall

The Windows Vista campaign we discuss in the introduction to this book left a lot of wreckage in its wake—as will any campaign botched as deeply and publicly as that one was. By the time the program had ended, though, your three authors had come out pretty clean on the other side. We'd gotten a few of the important things right, but we also got lucky with a lot of things beyond our control. The whole snafu produced a (mostly) thoughtful public discussion about how bloggers should handle similar programs in the future. The debate generated a default set of rules about transparency and integrity that still largely govern the blogosphere today (see WOMMA's Code of Ethics[5]). We can't and won't claim credit for that. In the middle of the whole firestorm, while we were scrambling to cover our butts, we had no way of knowing that the bloggers would work things out rather amicably and with a largely happy outcome.

We can and do take pride in how we handled the fallout that we could control. Microsoft, Acer, and AMD (but mostly Microsoft) got their fair share of criticism in all this, but so did some of the influencers who'd posted the earliest blogs and started to question the motives behind the whole giveaway. We made sure we maintained our connection to as many of those influencers as we could and did everything in our power to help them maintain their credibility and their audiences. We did this mainly by asking what we could do to help. We talked to the influencers on the warpath, as well as those beating a hasty retreat. We worked to help facilitate some sort of common ground amongst those who would listen.

Ultimately, both we and the bloggers came out the better for the whole experience. In our case, we were left with a long list of bloggers who could've jettisoned us for the trouble but whose attention we now had because we'd made sure to do whatever we could to keep them on our side. One was Long Zheng, the blogger caught at the epicenter of the whole debate. In fact, he was the first blogger to question the Vista giveaway on his blog, starting the entire string of events that generated millions of page views and even more publicity in traditional media over 72 subsequent hours. Here's what he wrote on his blog, IStartedSomething.com, when Chris left AMD to start up Ivy Worldwide: "I didn't know Chris very well, and it hurts me to say I've probably caused him the most trouble during his career at AMD. Some of you might remember that little misunderstanding of generosity at December of last year, if you don't, please don't look it up. I cannot imagine how much trouble that incident might have caused

Chris, but I sure didn't expect him to ever interact with me again. But Chris did. Not only is Chris interacting with me, he's even helping me. You see, I never got a computer, it's a long story. [But] I have a lot to thank Chris for." Similar sentiments popped up on many other blogs. We took one royal tumble on the Vista campaign, surely, but still managed to control the fall in the process, minimizing the damage and getting back up to rejoin the tussle.

Social media provides an incredible stage, as much for your gaffes as for your brilliant successes. It's the perfect venue for a company to trumpet its new products. It offers a massive audience—one that a marketer can leverage to help spread the word far beyond the theater itself—but such a stage can lay bare a company's dirty laundry, too. Actors no longer have the only roles in the performance. The audience will take over any production that's not honest, transparent, interesting, relevant, entertaining, or in some way useful to them. Worse yet, mistakes on the social-media stage happen in real time and in front of a worldwide audience. They don't just fade into the background like a forgotten word or missed cue; instead, they spread like wildfire, lingering in search-engine results for years.

As the emphasis on social media continues to increase, marketers will have to hit the gas to keep up. They'll have to address mistakes with much more urgency and earnestness than in the past. Decisions made to control a fall, minimize the damage, and get back up will have to happen simultaneously, or at least in very rapid succession. For those marketers who have adopted a social- and judo-like mindset, this will start to come as second nature; they will have learned how to react to falls. They will have learned that their industry's key influencers don't want to simply tear a company to shreds; they will find that they can count on those same influencers to help them get back up when things go awry.

We keep revisiting this point because we still get the same question every time we meet with a new company: What if they say something bad about us? Listen: "They" already are, and they're going to keep talking about you in both positive and negative ways, whether you join the conversation or not. Any company that has a product or service also has someone, somewhere saying something about it, and a few of those comments are bound to be negative. It's a fact of life, not just something suddenly brought about by the advent of social media. We live in a society that gives more attention to the negative and in which a critic always gets more attention for railing than the enthusiast does for waxing poetic.

What's more, the critics have driven marketers into their shells at the worst of times: just as social media is taking on an increasingly vital role in customers' buying decisions. Tealeaf Technology, Inc. and Harris Interactive have conducted an e-commerce survey in each of the past five years. In the 2009 poll, 76% of respondents said that negative comments online influenced their likelihood to do business with a company. That's not an especially encouraging statistic for companies already worried about jumping into social media, but the survey suggests that staying out of social media might be a worse idea. More than 8 out of 10 people said that social media influences their choice of vendor, suggesting that companies who build a robust presence in blogs and other social media avenues could gain an advantage. Further, more than half of all respondents said social media influenced their online transactions, and of those, slightly more people posted a good review (26%) than a bad one (21%).

Trends are changing even more rapidly post-purchase. The ratio of people who share their experiences directly with a company dropped to 66%, while the percentage of people sharing their experiences via blogs or other social media doubled to 12%. Furthermore, about 44% of the respondents said they posted comments on blogs and other social media because they hoped to influence others' buying decisions.

Of course, we can twist statistics to say a lot of things, but no one can deny that a growing number of customers want to and will seek out and engage in conversations about your products. They'll do it whether companies participate or not. They'll do it whether companies screw up or run without a hitch. And in both cases, the critics inevitably will have their say.

You could fill a library or two with all the books people have written about dealing with online criticism. We have no intention of plowing the same ground. Suffice it to say, companies no longer can get away with flippant justifications of their own or their products' deficiencies. How your company responds to problems now can make all the difference. Do you try to make things right, or do you try to justify it away? (Or worse, do you just ignore it, hoping it'll go away?) Depending on the situation, a company might need to admit it's wrong. Sometimes it has to become the aggressor and prove something false, and on some occasions, the company might do best just to listen and react only very carefully, in an orchestrated way. Different problems demand different responses. The constant is this: Companies that treat their customers' complaints earnestly and approach problems with honesty and transparency rarely fail over the long run. Jeanne Bliss, our friend and the author of *I Love You More Than My Dog*, puts it more bluntly: "If your company is not customer-centric, social media is not going to make any difference anyway."

For those companies that respect their customers, dealing with negative comments and criticism on the Web doesn't have to happen alone. As we covered in the prior chapter, we constantly work to strengthen our relationships with the key influencers in our clients' industries. We do it in good times and in bad times. Marketers who build those types of personal, well-established relationships in good times will discover something when things go sour: They have some powerful allies to help them recover when the tables turn, as tables are wont to do.

Those companies will get a fair shake from key influencers when the chips are down because they've proven themselves worthy of it. This is especially true because these relationships allow the company to make sure the influencers evaluate a product or service based on how well it meets identified customer need, and not just based on whether the influencer herself would buy it. Not every influential voice also squarely fits within the target market for a given product or service—so a truly influential voice has to distinguish between *what they want* and *what their readers need to know*. Far too many companies just throw products into the influencer's hands and say, "Tell me what you think." This recipe for complete disaster demonstrates an utter lack of understanding of how online influencers operate and has led to countless criticisms of those influencers and their methods.

Why? The fault lies largely with the company and its PR people, who simply want to gain any possible mention of the brand and then hope it's a positive mention. These woeful, half-baked and hasty attempts by most companies get nowhere, because the PR departments have no real relationships with influencers and no interest in a dialogue about the needs of the market and how a product or service meets those needs. As a result, the PR flak is left hoping, and what he gets is what he gets. Think of it this way: If you walked into a store and asked a sales person to hand you 10 items at random, how many of those items would you want to buy on the spot? There's no way you're going to like all 10 products, and chances are pretty good you'll want only three or four. Without the proper contextual understanding, the sales person can't identify and understand the products you need. So why would you expect your interactions with online influencers to be any different? If you don't ever ask, you can only guess at what influencers need—and more often than not, your guess will be wrong. If, on the other hand, you've already engaged them on their own terms, you'll know what they need. They'll be much more willing to work with you. They'll tell you *in private* how to fix a potential problem. They'll tell you where your offering falls short and will listen when you explain that it doesn't (of course, they'll make up their own minds in the end). They'll go public only when they feel that doing so is the only way to get the message out to the company.

The difference between the PR failures and a mutually beneficial relationship is dialogue, which underpins every aspect of our approach to social media. At Ivy Worldwide, we want all the influencers with whom we work to say, "Yeah, I know these guys and know they are a good company that generally gets it, and I can help them put this product on the right track." This doesn't mean the influencers will post blind, all-out defenses of the company and our clients, but it does mean they'll argue against unfair criticism; they'll help explain why things went wrong in design or execution, or, best of all, they might even help us avoid the mistake in the first place.

It's this third-party, independent support that can break up a storm of negative publicity—much more quickly and at much less expense than any company can do on its own. And you get it only when you already have the influencers on your side. Plus, with search ruling everything, a greater number of positive blog posts helps drive down negative results from the top of search engines. This online reputation management can help balance the top 20 or 30 results for most searches because blogs typically account for about 40% of the top search results for a company or brand.

Unintended Consequences

For many companies just tiptoeing into the world of word-of-mouth marketing, nothing knocks them off balance like the unpredictability of the social media landscape. In the churning chaos of blogs, ratings sites, forums, and the like, people often misinterpret a company's message, confuse its intentions, or tell outright lies about the firm and its products. As we noted above, the company that shifts its thinking and approaches social media with a truly social mindset will have influential allies who can help set the record straight.

Another subtle shift occurs when a company approaches social media with an open mind, however; the unintended consequences suddenly begin to work in its favor. In fact, the

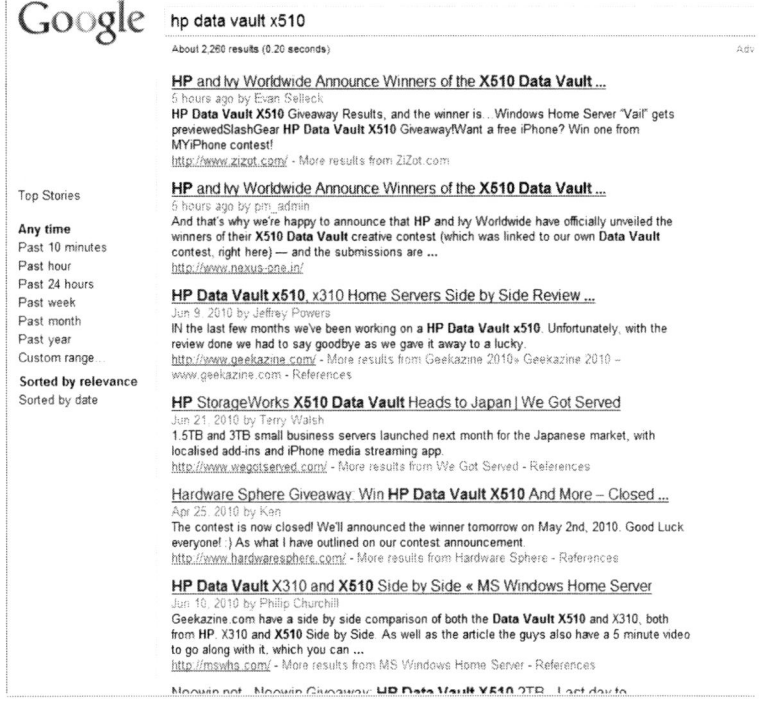

The first page of Google results for a campaign we did for HP's X510 Data Vault product. Even though HP had a wealth of pages already indexed by Google and had employed search engine-optimization (SEO) to all of these pages, the blogs we worked with accounted for 9 of the top 10 results in this example. This is why we often joke that BLOG stands for "Better Listings on Google."

company begins to anticipate the oddities as they arise and can work with influencers to turn them in its favor. But this doesn't happen without a complete and total mental shift, the adoption of an approach that's different from the traditional marketer's or PR's mindset. It means asking rather than telling. It means continually seeking buy-in from influencers and other advocates of the company and products. It means first asking how *it* can help *them*, and then following through on how influencers respond. Companies that do these things will have influencers readily working *with* them—not *against* them, and certainly not *for* them. Look for maximum efficiency with minimum effort, seek programs that provide benefits for all sides involved, and demonstrate you'll work with your best customers day in and day out. Make these tenets a fundamental part of your approach not just to social media, but to marketing in general, and circumstances will continually turn your way.

That's not to say that every single project will work famously, even with the right approach every time. We've slogged through some mediocre programs, too. Sometimes the timing isn't right. Sometimes the product or the pricing isn't right. More often, it's a combination of several things, as was the case with Chicbuds. Chicbuds put a fashionable spin on ear-bud headphones, placing crystals on the buds to up the style factor. They're cute and they work well enough, but they don't break any new ground for sound quality or fashion.

With the holiday shopping season approaching, the company hired us to generate some buzz for the product. We began researching the landscape of offerings and realized we had a challenge on our hands. As nice as the Chicbuds were, the $49 price tag seemed *way* too high. A comparable unadorned pair of earbuds, also made in Taiwan, sold for $4. We decided to focus on the style factor and hoped to offset the higher price with a buy-one, get-one-free promotion on Black Friday (the day after US Thanksgiving, generally one of the largest-volume shopping days in the year). One blogger's post got about 75,000 hits on that Friday, but it didn't drive sales. What's more, not a single person took up the buy-one, get-one-free offer on the blogs promoting it. The product's limited distribution, its high price, and customers' ease of substitution couldn't be overcome by a significant amount of traffic to the participating blogs. It wasn't out finest hour, but we had known even before beginning that the smartest approach to word-of-mouth marketing won't necessarily work for every product, especially when the product is deficient in some meaningful respect. In other words, we knew that social media won't disguise a campaign that ignores marketing's Four P's: product, price, place (distribution), and promotion.

The immaturity and rapid changes occurring in the world of social media don't make marketing decisions any easier. We spend much of our time figuring out which social media tools will work for certain products and programs, and we constantly study the landscape so we can identify the points where our clients' marketing cycles and the needs of our key influencers intersect. It's a full-time job, and one that inherently comes with risks, but there's simply no choice in the matter now that social media is a given for customers worldwide—we have to iterate and revise until we hit upon what works. Bottom line, marketers who aren't afraid to fail—the ones who have learned how to fall—will figure it out long before their competitors do.

Lessons From The Fall

Let's take another instructive trip down memory lane. Computer maker Dell had a social-media firestorm on its hands in 2005. For years, the company had consistently posted top scores on the University of Michigan's annual American Customer Satisfaction Index (ACSI). It had enjoyed a sterling reputation for quality service and support, regularly besting Apple, HP, and other competitors, but by the time 2005 rolled around, the company's constant push to reduce costs had started to erode its tech-support operations. Its scores on the ACSI had begun to slide, but only slightly—nothing that a little wise spending and some PR work couldn't fix.

Then, "Dell Hell" exploded onto the scene. Jeff Jarvis, a widely published essayist, started chronicling the problems he was having with a Dell notebook, posting the tale for everyone to read on his popular blog, BuzzMachine.com. His first post, in which he merely complained about the faulty PC and the hassle of sending it back for repairs, hit the Internet on June 21, 2005. It only got worse from there. Over the next month, Dell gave Jarvis the run-around. It botched service calls and gave Jarvis the typical stock, PR-sanctioned answers to his inquiries, so Jarvis made Dell his own special cause. By the time he was through, the blogosphere was littered with stories about Dell Hell.

During Jarvis' crusade, Dell responded only in fits and starts. But with its reputation for customer service getting torn to shreds and scattered across the blogosphere, the company finally reacted in full force. Spurred on by founder Michael Dell, the company created a social media team and started a series of corporate blogs. The new team went on its own crusade, joining the conversation and reaching out to customers who'd posted their problems online. The group would accept blame, help customers still having problems, and put a real, human face on the company. Once Dell's bitter enemy, Jarvis started writing blog posts that complimented the company for its efforts. Dell Hell became the prime example of what to do right—of how companies *should* engage their customers.

In *Word of Mouth Marketing*, Andy Sernovitz explains the shift in the PC maker's reputation: "Because Dell was one of the first companies to get called out for not listening to its word of mouth, it became one of the first companies to learn how to do it the right way." Sernovitz calls this "the power of making people happy." If an unhappy customer tells five people about his experience, an unhappy customer who is made happy again tells 10 people. "Fixing problems is the most powerful marketing you can do," Sernovitz writes.

Every fall inherently offers an opportunity to get back up. Marketers who adopt a mindset geared for social media inherently see the chance to reap rewards when the risks become reality. They can see the upside possible in the downside. We can launch into our projects with great confidence because we know we have dozens of allies throughout the blogosphere who can help to generate a wave of positive buzz or to counteract a wave of criticism.

Dell realized this, but only in retrospect. Theirs is a great example for how to handle the wave of negativity. The company dealt very well with fixing problems and correcting its negative buzz. It created a place for customers to complain directly to them instead of across the Web. Dell took a proactive approach to finding those complaints posted on the Web and addressing them individually. It gradually started turning negatives into neutrals and neutrals into positives. It even launched IdeaStorm, a forum where customers could post and vote on ideas for Dell's product development.

The company deserves credit for its ultimate reaction to Dell Hell, but we'd be remiss if we didn't note that its approach also stands as a great lesson in unintended consequences. Today, Dell has trapped itself in a limited approach to the social media landscape, one that forces them to expend too much time and energy and do too much work on its own. Its corporate blogs have become Dell's default answer for almost every social media campaign. And when it comes down to the point of all this, driving sales, the company's market share hasn't recovered since it declined in 2007. In fact, Dell lost its title of world's largest PC maker by volume to HP in 2007, and it fell to No. 3 behind Acer in 2009.

IdeaStorm poses yet more problems. Although we love any idea that brings valuable customer feedback into the product-development cycle, welcoming every customer (or potential customer) to comment and treating each one equally results in a lot of energy wasted in separating the wheat from the chaff. Within days of announcing the IdeaStorm site, Dell was overrun by comments from the Linux community, which wanted the company to pre-load and support the open-source operating system on its consumer PCs. Dell started selling consumer models with the Ubuntu version of the Linux software, a decision that sparked a loud cheer from the open-source community but little else. Sales of the Ubuntu-equipped models ultimately never took off.

Dell has touted the fact that it has sold $3 million of PCs via Twitter over a year and a half. Although on the surface this seems to be one more shining example of a company really using social media (especially Twitter) to make money, the truth is a little different. A *Wall Street Journal* article on the story revealed that according to Dell, they employ 200 plus individuals in their social-media efforts, including driving sales via

Twitter. With low profit margins in the PC business (about 5% to 7%), Dell would have to sell $3 billion of PCs *each year* to cover the cost of all of these employees and their benefits.__

All that being said, launching a line of PCs running Linux or selling PCs via Twitter is not a bad thing. And don't get us wrong—at the time they were launched, many of Dell's initiatives did the trick. The company has done a remarkable job of getting out ahead of its rivals, forcing them to scramble and catch up with Dell's social-media efforts, but it has also bogged itself down with overhead because it failed to adopt a judo-like philosophy that would have leveraged the Web's momentum and engaged a broad collection of the PC industry's key influencers. Dell has allowed other computer makers, HP in particular, to capitalize on the rapidly changing social-media landscape and establish their own advantages. Do you know of any other company with similar margins that would be willing and able to commit more than 200 employees to an effort and not show a profit or market-share growth several years into the game?

Because the social media ecosystem is still largely a land grab and continues changing so rapidly, thoughtful marketers have a rare and golden opportunity to place their companies well ahead of competitors. They can craft online word-of-mouth campaigns that force their competitors to react defensively instead of blazing their own trails. Those chances don't happen often, and they don't last forever. In this day and age, in the hyper-mediated world of the Internet, it takes the proper social mindset to create a sustainable advantage—and, of course, a firm grasp on the basics of social-media marketing.

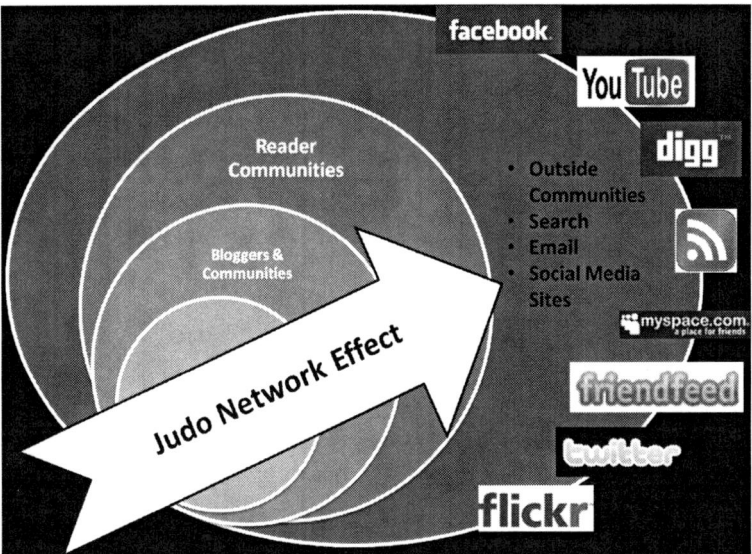

Influencers grow and engage their audiences by linking to each other as well as by pushing content out to social-media platforms like Twitter and Facebook, where they usually have more fans, friends, or followers than the brands they cover.

CHAPTER 4

Uchikomi:
Mastering The Basics

UNDESERVEDLY, JOHN OBETO DOESN'T GET the marquee treatment of better-known bloggers. Few among the millions of people who visit Gizmodo or Engadget have even heard of or visited John's blog, AbsolutelyWindows.com. Computer-technology companies will look at the online traffic figures and skip right past him—and they'll miss out on one of the most influential bloggers in one of the most difficult-to-reach markets.

Obeto doesn't have a huge audience, but he's one of the few influencers who writes a blog specifically and only about small- to mid-size business (SMB) computing issues. He has a fraction of the audience of the biggest blogs, which focus on general technology or consumer computing. He's one of the most positive and concise writers we know, yet he has to work his tail off to get companies to talk to him. Those that look at his site and take the time to find out what he's about, however, will discover what we eventually found: His content and audience are pure gold.

Almost all of Obeto's readers are prime customers for tech companies, which spend a lot of time and effort trying to find and market to this group. SMB customers make up one of the largest customer pools, but it's a pool that's fractured and often difficult to reach. Rather than finding one customer to spend $100,000, companies have to find 100 customers who will each spend $1,000. Nevertheless, groups of small- and midsize business customers will congregate in certain areas where they can find solid advice, and Obeto's AbsolutelyWindows.com is one of those gathering areas.

There's a significant lesson in all this: When seeking out the key influencers in any industry, companies have to look well beyond traffic numbers. They have to discover the true value of the content producers who influence their customers, and they have to understand those online conversations at both micro and macro levels. It's one of the basic skills any marketer must possess, but when being applied online, the skill requires that shift in mindset that's seemingly so elusive. A marketer must look at what really defines influence, because it's far more than just page views. Whether out of laziness, budget or time constraints, or simple naiveté, many marketers will simply think the bigger, the better. As our experience has shown us time and time again, however, the number of page views *does not* equal influence or driving sales. Engadget.com might reprint a snippet of your press release (or, more likely, some other site's mention of it) with a snarky comment relevant to only a very small fraction of its readers. In contrast, AbsolutelyWindows.com will use your product over a long period of time and in a context relevant to the target market. By providing the kind of insight that engages virtually all its small business readers, John and bloggers like him cater to specific markets and niches that lead to a significant bearing on actual purchasing decisions.

The fundamental shift in mindset that we've repeatedly mentioned has to happen before any of these skills work, but thinking only generates sales when it's accompanied by action. In judo, a master develops the most basic skills so he or she can react quickly when precision is most important, and, like a judo practitioner, a marketer gains expertise only through repeated practice of fundamental marketing skills. In both pursuits, building expertise with the basic tools is essential to understanding how and why certain techniques work and others fail. A marketing group that doesn't invest the time and energy in learning and mastering the basics—such as identifying the real influencers in their market and finding mutually beneficial ways to engage them—will pass over a guy like John Obeto out of sheer ignorance.

We have seen too many companies and marketing agencies blame the program or fault social media for their lack of success (remember the Toshiba example where they copied 31 Days of the Dragon). The company that doesn't shift its mindset will simply go on along the path of least resistance, continually missing opportunities to drive sales. They will open windows for their competitors to step in and ultimately force the company into catch-up mode. We see this every time we make a presentation at a trade show or conference. We get the same questions every time:

- How did you find these influencers?

- Why did you choose these bloggers?

- Why didn't you work with this (fill in the blank) blog?

- We tried something like this, so why didn't it work as we expected?

When we help and address their questions and concerns, almost every time, these skilled marketers say some version of the following: "We had tried this X number of times and could not figure out what was wrong or why we were not getting the results that we expected or that you did." The amazing thing is not that they keep trying the same thing over and over and expecting different results but that from the beginning, their mindset was wrong and that led them down the same path. It was as if their compass pointed south instead of north and helped push every turn in the wrong direction.

Customer Co-Marketing: Design And Development

It's common knowledge that social media has changed the way customers interact with brands and companies. Customers are now far more involved with the brands they care about, possessing a megaphone that can reach a worldwide audience. They research their purchases more, primarily because it's so easy to do. As noted by the McKinsey report we mentioned in Chapter 1, the placement of the right information in the right place can be the key to gaining a new customer, and it can be equally vital to retaining current customers' loyalties. To succeed, companies have to integrate a well-thought-out, mutually beneficial social media strategy into all phases of the marketing cycle.

We have a chart we use in almost every presentation we deliver. It draws out what we call the Influencer Cycle, which illustrates how a company can leverage its industry's key influencers throughout all phases of a product's life cycle. It starts with product and concept development, moves through design and field testing, then moves into executing a proactive go-to-market phase that intimately incorporates influencers and their audiences, ultimately winding up in a post-launch phase intended to maintain sales momentum while improving customers' service and support experiences.

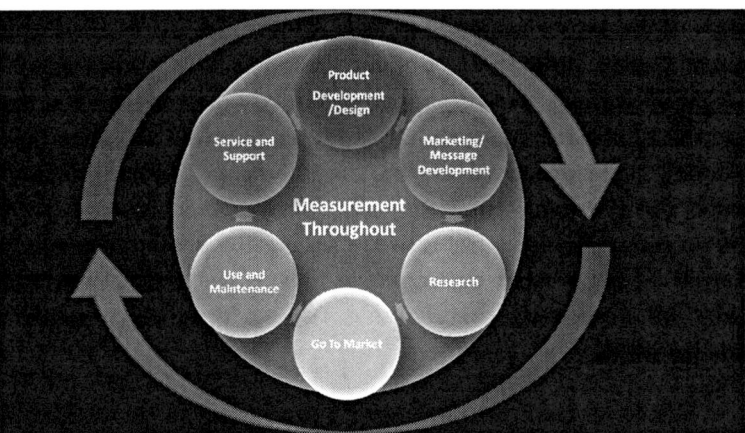

Social Media Judo is not just for new product introductions. The principles can be applied throughout the entire lifecycle of a product as well as used to improve and differentiate the company as a whole.

During a product's pre-launch stage, influencers can provide a host of intelligent and insightful development information. A blog's audience can provide a remarkably responsive focus group, one that's disproportionately engaged with the market because the market is their passion. (Traditional focus groups rarely, if ever, engage customers who share the same passion for a particular industry, technology, or type of product, which is why products designed mainly via focus-group input largely end up receiving lukewarm receptions, being viewed as having been "designed by committee.") Furthermore, syndicated research does not offer a competitive advantage because any competitor who can foot the bill has access to the same intelligence. Influencers provide far better pre-design input, drawing upon their own and their collective audience's experience and passion for an industry and its offerings. In fact, this applies to not only product design but also message formulation: Influencers are well positioned to help absorb the value proposition and refashion it into something that the target audience is more likely to respond to.

If the reason for a product's existence is to meet a customer need, doesn't it make sense to talk to the most interested members of the target audience to learn what those needs are? And once you've built your product, isn't that very same super-engaged segment best equipped to tell you how to position the product for maximum impact? To top it all off, if the most passionate representatives of your target market actually helped *build* the product, won't they also be the most fervent of its advocates, rallying to the cause of selling the product they help build? This is what customer co-marketing is all about, and why it's absolutely *essential* that you harness social media's innate value.

We have done word-of-mouth marketing or as we like to call it "customer co-marketing" on behalf of numerous clients; the clearest example was the tx1000/tx2000 design program we ran with HP. When HP introduced one of the first affordable tablet PCs, the tx1000, the market started to take a fresh look at tablet PCs. The bloggers we worked with liked the tx1000 overall but said it could use some changes. Rather than simply ignore them or shine them on, we created a formal program to capture their feedback and give them a role in designing the next version, the tx2000.

At the same time, Dell was launching several new notebooks that came in different colored shells. The press was applauding Dell's design focus for this initiative. Many of the people at HP and most bloggers saw the spray-painted notebooks as nothing new and not worthy of design accolades. Using this knowledge, we launched a campaign to showcase the new HP designs at Chris Pirillo's Gnomedex conference, where more than 500 of the leading bloggers from all segments, interests, and topics get together to discuss the state of the blogosphere. This venue provided us with ready access to virtually every segment of the blog world and a forum to ask them what they wanted in a notebook from HP. More than that, however, we used it as way to show off HP's newest designs (many had not seen in the flesh) and to get HP credit for, as one blogger later put it, "real design and not just a Krylon paint job."

The campaign was simple:

- Get credit for HP for the design and launch of the tx1000
- Ask more than 500 bloggers and influencers to tell HP what features they want in a notebook/tablet
- Build a forum for the bloggers and HP to share ideas (done in Ivy Worlwide's private forum, IN Network)
- Bring in HP's design team to show how and why features and design elements are added to final products, showcasing the latest generation of HP notebooks
- Set the stage for the bloggers to get credit for helping design the tx2000 tablet launching at the Consumer Electronics Show

The results speak for themselves:

- HP used the feedback to develop the tx2000 as well as other HP designs.
- HP got valuable insight on competitors from people who review more than 150 computers and other technology products each year
- Influencers took credit for the HP design and helped launch the tx2000, calling it "a product we helped build."
- A real relationship of listening and a true mutual-admiration society was begun between HP and influencers.
- We were enabled to run other programs with these and other influencers.
- Content including posts, video, and audio on HP's designs was seen by more than 30 million consumers during the first two months of the campaign.

We should also mention that all of this was done without sharing non-public or confidential information with the bloggers. By asking what they wanted and what they liked about HP and other companies' offerings, we were able to give feedback on the ideas and thoughts they had without showing the final product until launch day. This enabled the design team to get all of the information it wanted without embargoing 500 bloggers. At launch, the design team credited the bloggers for their suggestions and feedback and pointed out specific features, technologies, or other elements in the final product that the bloggers had a hand in bringing about. Win-win for everyone.

Customer Co-Marketing: Go To Market

The examples we've given thus far have focused on the proactive process of enfranchising influencers in designing and developing a product to ensure maximum market success. This may be biting off too much for many companies at this stage of the evolution of social media, however, so it may make more sense to focus on selling today's offerings. In this case, the influencer's role is to get the message out to the target customer in a rapid and compelling fashion and to help drive sales. With an approach that offers mutual benefit to the influencer (usually including, but not necessarily limited to, improving site traffic), an influencer-centric marketing campaign supporting a product launch will generate a wave of content with third-party credibility hand-delivered to your target market. This content may consist of product reviews, forum threads, tweets, videos, podcasts, or all of the above. In many cases, this wave of content builds on itself, generating yet more content and discussion and creating a wealth of endorsement coupled with referral to your sales channels. At its best, such a campaign goes viral and becomes a sort of a mini pop-culture hit. At the least, a properly designed and executed influencer-marketing campaign will improve your product's search-engine rankings and increase the level of discussion around it on your industry's most important blogs and Web sites.

Customer Co-Marketing: Post-Purchase Support

Inevitably, the buzz of a product launch begins to tail off shortly after launch; however, the role of social media in driving awareness, sales, and customer satisfaction doesn't have to end after launch and, as in many cases, before the product hits shelves. Working with forums like Neowin.net (one of the best sources for PC help and advice on the Internet), a company can help provide technical support and aftermarket service for its customers at a fraction of traditional costs, merely by enfranchising influencers from the outset. A well-timed contest—or even just an extended discussion of how to use or get more out of your product or service—can extend the buzz, for both your offering and the influencers' readers. The reason for this is that once an influential voice has endorsed a product, it becomes one of the most readily accessible avenues for support after a reader has purchased. Customers tend to be very pragmatic in this respect: If a site owner has a lot of experience with a product, he or she probably also knows how to help get the most out of it. They'll help ensure their readers have a good experience, partly to solidify their own credibility and partly to increase preference for their site. Aside from driving down support costs, working with these influencers helps marketers quickly understand how the product is being received and where additional marketing or support issues may lie. It is this strategy of constant influencer enfranchisement that will reinvigorate your products and messages, as well as your relationships with the bloggers — and, by extension, your customers.

Tying It All Together

It takes a company-wide commitment to make your marketing process work throughout the product lifecycle. A company has to be willing and committed to making social media an integral part of its entire agenda of marketing activities. Social media can't be merely an add-on, or a separate program rolled out as an afterthought, or simply a throwing-money-and-people-at-the-problem approach (like our Dell example). For your company to extract maximum value from social media, social media must permeate the entire marketing discipline. We generally say 60% of a company's social-media efforts should amplify traditional marketing efforts. The remaining 40% should consist of activities specifically designed for the social-media world alone, such as sponsoring influencer-centric promotions, incorporating influencers into events, or repurposing influencer-generated content into your own outbound marketing. Bolt on a little social media at the end of the marketing plan, and you're bound to produce mediocre results at best.

Of course, none of the internal integration of social media means much if the company doesn't master the basics of influencer identification and outreach as well. Working with key influencers to help launch a product but ignoring the influencers' advice for product development and campaign evaluation will lead to you missing out on fully exploiting the opportunity to create a sustainable advantage that ultimately will allow you to outpace the competition.

Making Contact

Marketing requires interaction with other people, whether customers, partners, colleagues, or all of the above. But for some reason, add the idea of social media and the possibility of a public marketplace of ideas, and the interactions seem much more threatening, at least to the unschooled. They need not be this way. With a modicum of careful study and consideration—and a little help from some new friends—a company can find the right people with whom to co-market its products. The three basics to master don't pose an impossible challenge, especially when one approaches them from a fundamentally social mindset.

1. Identify your company's and industry's key online influencers
2. Work toward building long-term personal and professional relationships with those influencers
3. Tap in to the influencers' expertise and collective audience by asking them questions instead of taking them demands

Each of these steps will require time, energy, and, above all, know-how, but once you start to cycle through these steps, you'll find that your marketing efforts will be turbocharged by this new network of friends.

Identify Your Key Influencers

When people think of the hot products that light up the blogosphere today, it's safe to say they don't think of scissors, but as John Moore can tell you, every company has its fanatics, and Fiskars has found a novel way to energize them through social media. "Can you get a more boring product than a pair of scissors?" asks Moore, the founder of Brand Autopsy and the official WOMMA enthusiast. "But what Fiskars did brilliantly well was realize that scrap-bookers loved to use their orange-handled scissors because it gives a masterful cut. Lo and behold, they tap into this customer fan base. ... So they built the Fisk-A-Teers. The company realized it might make products that are somewhat boring, but it has fans out there that can spread the word on what it means to design better scrapbooks." And to those who *really* care about scrapbooking, isn't this all that matters?

Fiskars gathered some ardent scrapbookers, dubbed them "crafting ambassadors," and started them blogging at Fiskateers.com. As a community started forming around the blog, Moore says, it gave Fiskars a chance to hear what real customers were saying about its products. They could use the audience as a focus group of prime customers, sharing ideas and getting feedback on new products. And Fiskars builds that feedback into their product-design process. "If a company, no matter what it is, does something that earns an opinion," Moore says, "people are going to talk about it."

We like this example because it shows that no matter who you are or what you build, your company can do this—provided it finds the right influencers. Fiskars turned its community leaders into a stable of influencers from whom it could extract insights and with whom it could collaborate time and again. What's more, these super-engaged industry experts afford a degree of authority and authenticity that only a third-party endorsement can provide. The key is finding the right people who are enthusiastic about your product or industry and enfranchising them in the process of building, selling, and supporting your products, because that's what they really want, being the enthusiasts they are, and many of them are already doing some of all of this anyway.

Identifying these influencers doesn't have to be difficult, but it does take some homework. Several companies sell products or services that help firms track the online conversations that mention a brand, product, or company. These tracking services have gotten much more sophisticated in recent years, even to the point of being able to use natural-language logic to distill the ratio of positive to negative comments. They are a good start, but a more sophisticated approach is required to yield a broad-enough and deep-enough perspective on the right influencers to engage. The John Obetos of the world won't jump off the page if you rely solely on tracking software or a quick Web search. Go to the conferences that matter to your industry and find the bloggers who not only have something to say but are shaping the conversation within the industry. Ask the influencers you know whose sites they read, or who they see as competition for their audiences. Read all those blogs. Then read them again. Read the comments, too—and even dare to post a few when you can contribute to this conversation. Read all the blogs to which they link, and read the ones that link to those. Eventually, you'll find your company's and industry's key influencers.

Also, let's be clear about how many influencers you really need to work with, and why a little goes a long way. For most companies, the list will be 20 to 40 or 50 key bloggers or influencers. Yes, that's right, *as few as 20 can do the job*. Remember, you're striving for maximum results with minimum effort. If you chose the right 20 to 40 people that other influencers follow and who also cover all of your target markets and segments, this will be all you really need. Remember 31 Days of the Dragon had, well, 31 influencers. In fact, across five of HP's lines of business (consumer and commercial notebooks and desktops, as well as servers), they work with fewer than 150 total influencers. This includes horizontal and vertical targets as well as key demographics like college, fashion, female-centric, and Hispanic and other niche markets. So, unless you are as big as HP and serve as many markets as it does, you should be fine with 20 or so influencers, at least to get the ball rolling. Plus, think of it this way: Can you or your department really have a truly one-to-one relationship with more than that anyway?

Develop The Relationship

The toughest part for marketers stuck in the traditional mindset is developing and cultivating these relationships for the long haul. We've seen a lot of our brothers and sisters jump into social media and get caught up in all its similarities to the traditional, PR-driven approach. One still crafts a message as part of an integrated marketing campaign and, ultimately, tries to create a program that influences the greatest possible number of people and incites them to buy your product, but unlike TV, print, or other marketing communications channels, social media inherently involves *personal* interactions—in all their phases and at all times. This is inescapable, and it means you absolutely *have* to forge longstanding, ongoing relationships with the bloggers and content producers who influence your customers, because they have the potential to influence thousands of those customers *at any time*.

"Our interest has always been in long-term growth and not these short-term growth spurts," says Rob Bushway, the former editor of GottaBeMobile.com. "The thing that Ivy Worldwide does that helps, is their work is more than a one-time blip. They've built a long-term relationship between us and their clients. This affords us early access to products. It's access to images and a beta ahead of time. It's us giving feedback and them taking it to heart." That sounds like common sense, but it doesn't fit with the traditional marketing frame of mind. A marketer has to begin by thinking about *what bloggers want*, and *not* what he or she wants to get from the bloggers. Online influencers tend to be type-A personalities; they blog because they are passionate about the topic or category and they feel compelled to share their knowledge with others who feel the same way they do. They're on this planet to generate traffic, whether it is via video, text, Twitter, or Facebook, for their brands and for themselves. Once a marketing group spends time reading these influencers and talking with them, enabling them becomes the obvious choice. Help them generate content that puts their brands and your company in the best possible light. That's the first step of training for your judo social-media black belt.

After that, marketers can start to think tactically about the different content that each influencer produces. Marketers can mix and match the more subtle pieces of a marketing campaign to both fit the needs of different influencers and reach a certain customer segment. They can start to identify which bloggers are best positioned to help engage particular target segments. This also helps the influencers with their objectives by enabling them to produce the content that will drive traffic to their sites and further engagement with their readers. A blogger who focuses on small business, such as John Obeto, can help a company reach the market and do so in a more credible way than the company can ever aspire to, just as Bushway can help reach the road warrior in the same credible way.

We have yet to find a category or topic that does not have an influential group of bloggers engaging the market and sharing their passion with other who feel the same way. Your job is to find them, get to know them, and give them what they need to build and grow their audiences. Companies that don't do this, or that do it only halfway, will alienate the very people who hold sway over a swath of customers. Take it from Jason Dunn: "Let's say all I want is information about laptops, but instead Company X has one giant email list for anyone who might cover their products. So I either have to drink from the fire hose, ignore them or get my news secondhand," Dunn says. "The days of all-or-nothing mailing lists are long gone. I think so many companies are still stuck in the '90s, when they faxed out news to everyone. But the Internet has allowed the creation of niches everywhere, so you end up with web sites just about netbooks, or just about HP netbooks, or even just one model of HP netbook. So if Company X doesn't segment in this way, if they don't specialize each of their communications to their customer segments, they risk pushing away the bloggers – people like me. Over time, that can actually generate *negative* feedback and lose support from the exact group they are try to connect with."

Give The People What They Want

We won't sugarcoat it: It takes a committed investment of time and energy to decipher how a company can benefit from the blogosphere and to learn which influencers can have the broadest impact on a product, service, or support initiative. Frankly, most companies that want to go from mediocre to best in class are better off finding an experienced expert or agency that focuses on this, but for those who go it alone, we offer this bit of advice: Always remember that you're not in it alone. If you get stumped by a problem, run into a dead end, or just don't know how to approach a topic, just ask. A company that identifies its key influencers has a list of experts at its fingertips. A marketer who has gone out of her way to develop relationships with those content producers has a set of friends who'll be happy to help at a moment's notice.

The worst thing a marketer can do is try to cram a program into the blogosphere. Those who do try risk a very nasty reception. Ask, don't tell, because those who take the time to listen to their industries' influencers will have a wealth of market information at their fingertips. We owe 75% of our success to the advice, insight, and aid of the influencers with whom we work (the other 25% is solid training in the fundamentals of marketing). The difference, as Joel Evans, founder of Geek.com, says, is a personal approach: "That's always been [Ivy Worldwide's] approach – very friendly, never stuff it down your throat. They're also open to ideas: 'This is the message we're trying to deliver; make it work however your audience is open to seeing it.'" But far too many of the companies pitching to the Joel Evanses of the world don't get this simple point. It might be arrogance or ignorance, but it's a surefire recipe for failure, either way. "It's still stuck in first gear," he says. "I'll get pitches that say, 'Here are some unique products for your back-to-school guide.' We don't do a back-to-school guide. ... Just send me the product. I have a different audience than that. I'll look at it, and if I think it's interesting, I'll request it. It's a lot more about knowing the person and the blog you're pitching to than these companies think."

A blogger can't build or grow an audience with content that readers don't want to see. No one will watch a YouTube video channel if they have no interest in the topic at hand. Give them the information they can use. Like Evans says, if a site owner wants to write a review, send the site owner the product, but first, get to know him or her and the audience so you can position the product in a context, as this can help predispose the blogger to viewing the product positively. Then, give the the blogger the information he or she can use, ensuring that he or she will have a good experience with the product. In return, the blogger will be far more likely to give you feedback, guide you to his or her audience (i.e., your customers), and defend you from unfair criticism.

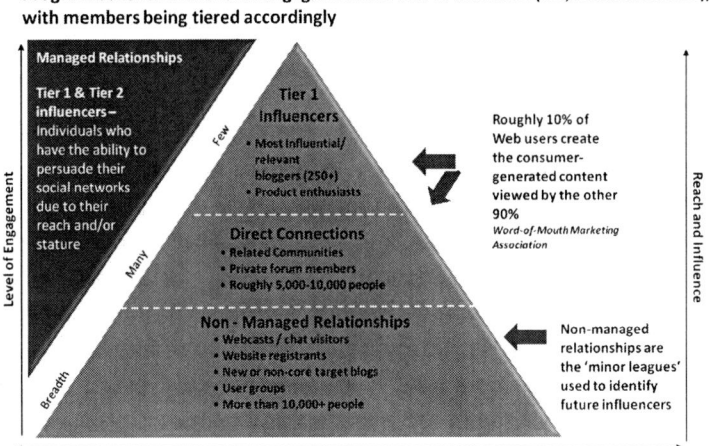

Program benefits and level of engagement are tied to influence (i.e., reach & stature), with members being tiered accordingly

Targeting the top of the pyramid (as opposed to the bottom like most companies do) enables you to build deep relationships with a few key bloggers who influence not only your customers but also other bloggers.

Robert Scoble and Shel Israel offer an interesting example of this phenomenon in their seminal 2006 book, *Naked Conversations*. In the book, they mention Randy Tinseth, who writes his "Randy's Journal" blog for Boeing, where he's vice president of marketing (www.boeingblogs.com/randy). In his journal, Randy chronicles the news at Boeing and tells stories about his travels in support of the company's commercial aviation group. His was among the earliest corporate blogs, and he typically

Judo Social Media Framework	The Influencers The New Media	The Followers	The Buyers
Who are they?	Top 1% of market like bloggers or super-engaged consumers	Top 10% any market like forum members or your core customers	The other 90% or any other consumers/buyers
How many is this usually?	Top 100 to 250+	Top 5000+	Rest of the World
What is the type of relationship?	1 to 1	1 to Many	Many to Many
What do they do?	Start conversations	Carry and promote conversations	Read and drive conversations
What do they want? What will they do for us?	Why now, why you, why are you better? Start/Tell and deliver the story/topic	Look at this? What is your take on this? How does this compare? Re-tell the story as their own and pass it along in their way to the masses	What should buy? What should I consider? Has anyone tried this? Participate in the conversation and bring more people in over time
How do they see themselves?	Brand/category ambassadors/defenders	The informed whose job it is help	Buyers wanting to make the right/smart choice
What is their role? What role do they serve?	Education: Writers The new media	Evangelists: Copy & paste, with comment The town criers	Empathy: Readers, consumers and buyers Consumers/buyers and future influencers
What do I need to do to work with them? How do I engage them?	Enfranchise them/make them part of the design/program ASAP Use to/for/with methodology to get them to deliver the story/topic	Identify their communities & vehicles – be where they are Use to/for/with methodology to get them to deliver the story/topic	Figure out what you want them to feel? How you want them to act? Give them something worth discussing and keep it going any way possible

The table above shows how the levels of the pyramid from the previous graphic interrelate and gives details on each stratum.

provided readers with some new information or an interesting story, but for the longest time that was all he did. The blog initially didn't allow comments, and even now, little real discussion happens at the site. Tinseth is a good writer, and he has some interesting stories to tell, but although his blog is more interactive than it used to be, it still doesn't generate much of an exchange with Boeing's customers (and it remains the only blog listed at boeingblogs.com, despite the name's plural connotation).

Despite this, Boeing has engaged the blogosphere in some very interesting ways, as Scoble and Israel note in their book. At one point, Boeing invited some of its industry's key influencers to ride along on the test flight of a 777, asking that they blog about the experience. The postings, Scoble and Israel wrote, were "universally favorable and passionate." In this case, Boeing's decision to provide influencers with a unique, hands-on, insider's look at the ongoing development of the 777 gave bloggers an event they could easily and naturally translate into content for their sites—content that was sure to drive traffic. That's what online publishers ultimately want: content that will keep current readers coming back while attracting new ones. Giving influencers the inside scoop helps them expand their audience and is usually not just off-the-record information. Rather, these scoops provide a behind-the-scenes view of the company, product, or topic that's otherwise impossible see and is exactly what a brand's fans want. Providing influencers with things to give away will help them further expand their audiences. Sending them a product early in its release cycle so they can have a review online when it launches will help increase their appeal and timeliness, thus assisting in expanding their readership. It's pretty simple: Companies have to give bloggers and other online publishers something they can *use*.

"'We'll give you five of these to give away' is a much better approach than 'I have this pre-canned idea of how this should run on your Web site and engage your readers,'" says Joel Evans. "That's a surefire way of alienating a lot of content producers. Everyone has their own style, and they have their own following because of that style. Some of the campaigns give us a little more promotion. But most important, is this something the reader would want to participate in? What's the true value? I can't tell you how many things arrive on my doorstep that no one would want. We're just *not* going to offer our readership a special deal on something like towels. They're expecting a certain quality and appeal from an offer."

Looking In

Marketing through social media remains an imprecise art. Campaigns fail for reasons a marketer has no way of predicting. Other campaigns might succeed despite a company's most inept fumbling when implementing it. One thing will *guarantee* failure, however: treating social media as a gimmick and just bolting it onto a marketing campaign without forethought. As the Web influences more and more purchasing decisions among buyers and customers, companies will have to fully integrate social media into their marketing departments. It's much easier to build an elevator into a building from the ground up than to add the elevator once the building has been built. More importantly, though, social media can help optimize most of the marketing department's other functions.

We break down the marketing cycle into three phases: pre, pro, and post. In the pre-marketing phase, companies can use social media to solicit feedback on product development, to test marketing messages, and to seed different stories with all types of media. For example, we often ask influencers to join an advisory board or to leverage knowledge of their audience to help us compile an especially effective, insightful, and passionate set of marketing messages. You might not think it, but gathering product intelligence during the pre-marketing phase is one of the best ways to create a competitive advantage for your product. This enables the influencers to be part of the development, and they therefore want to be part of the launch. Do this throughout your product portfolio and company and you'll find yourself in a newly competitive position as a result. We've seen it happen—better yet, we've helped orchestrated it.

The opportunities to capitalize on relationships with influencers naturally become much more apparent during the pro-marketing phase, whose start coincides with the product's launch in the marketplace. Here we start amplifying many of the outbound communications by marrying them with word-of-mouth marketing. For instance, we'll enact advertising and search-engine optimization efforts as well as media and channel programs. This includes securing product reviews and other third-party endorsements from influencers, prompting the production of consumer-generated media, and aligning with various affiliate programs that are designed to link content back to the product's sales channels. Keep in mind, however, that this stage also includes soliciting feedback on the product and gathering insight into the bevy of real-world technical-support issues that consumers are so well known for discovering and certain activities that are germane to social media alone, such as conducting influencer-devised promotional campaigns, come into play during this period. The entire marketing department should be on the clock during this phase, making use of influencer input in every conceivable fashion.

The post-marketing phase continues the charge into the marketplace by enhancing the customer's post-sales experience, making customer service available anywhere, in any language, and at any time, the world over. Although we call this "ubiquitous tech support," the outward, word-of-mouth communication function can still play an especially vital role here. As the buzz of the product launch begins to fade—and marketers are still charged with affecting sales—the residual effect of all those blog postings, ratings, evaluations, and extended discussions can continue to influence buyers well into the final stages of the product's lifespan. Contests designed and executed by influencer communities (campaigns such as the 31 Days of the Dragon and HP Magic Giveaway, which we will discuss later) can keep the conversation going well after the excitement of the launch wanes. More important, though, by giving communities ever more reason to discuss its products, a company can maintain momentum and potentially gain ground over its competitors, setting the competitive tenor and putting competitors in the position of continually play catch-up.

We've seen more companies start to integrate social media cross the entire marketing cycle, and that's a good thing, but we've seen precious few companies that have placed oversight of social-media efforts into the hands of anyone above a mid-level manager. Social media will never become an integral part of designing, launching, and supporting a product if it continues to be the responsibility of someone who can't see and isn't accountable for the big picture. Jeanne Bliss says that every company should have a customer-service vice president, or something akin to a chief customer-support officer. Better yet, every company should make it the job of every executive to ensure that its customers remain critical stakeholders in an organization's decision making, rather than the afterthought status that they usually are afforded. We think that an executive-level position should oversee social media and that the person in this position should direct how the company applies social media throughout its marketing cycle.

We recently visited two different organizations in Austin, one a large not-for-profit firm and the other, an educational institution. The two meetings started out in remarkably similar ways. We started each with a little light conversation, and then out it came: "We want to do social media." And that was that.

We started laughing. "Great," we said, "we're happy to help. But what are your goals and objectives? How do we make social media a part of your overall marketing and not just a one-off endeavor?" Most companies, especially those that are brand-new to social media and particularly risk-averse, go the one-off route—and it almost always ends up not working out as they'd hoped, causing them to abandon the entire experiment. Other companies question the return on investment of a single initial program without looking for the value it can bring over the long haul. Worst of all, some companies claim success for just having made the effort, regardless of the value of the outcome.

A proper social media strategy won't fuel success on its own—the Web's viral sensations are too few and far between (and usually come about completely by chance). Nevertheless, a well-thought-out and -executed social-media strategy *can* become a self-funding proposition. A proper social media strategy should amplify everything else a company does, and it should accomplish a few things that only social media can deliver. In one way, it's another arrow in the marketing quiver, one that can make all your other arrows fly longer, straighter, and more accurately. Show us a social media program, and we'll show you dozens of ways it can improve virtually everything else your company does. Properly integrated and executed, a social-media campaign becomes a boon to a company's marketing cycle, from start to finish.

Product Development

It should go without saying, but we'll say it anyway: None of our advice works if a company tries to sell a terrible product and provides terrible service. Jeanne Bliss put a whole new dimension on this with her book *Chief Customer Officer.* Her follow-on book, *I Love You More Than My Dog*, takes the idea of customer service a step further. Companies, she says, have to earn the right to their customers' continuing patronage. The same holds when the marketing moves online. "You have to earn the right to having social media have the biggest impact," she told us in an interview. "Everyone wants to get the rave, but you have to earn the rave first. You can't leap over the blocking and tackling of being a great company. If you do the rest of the basic stuff first, social media will fly you to the moon."

Nothing will get an influencer as jazzed as a cool new product. Sometimes writing a critical review can be a lot more fun, but for people truly interested in a particular industry, the innovations produced by its leading companies are what really moves them. Moreover, they like the idea of playing a part in driving the industry forward. *You can capitalize on this.* A company that brings its influencers into the product-development process from the outset will discover a fount of information about what its customers really want.

Dell hit on a brilliant idea, at least in theory, when it launched IdeaStorm to solicit feedback from its customers. In practice, the effort quickly turned into a mess, being taken over by Linux enthusiasts and others in their hundreds with half-baked ideas that had no hope of ever making it into a product sold by a company Dell's size. Instead, a firm that entertains the feedback of its influencers gets more wheat and less chaff. An influencer can tell product developers what the customer really wants, and in ways that the customer cannot possibly be expected to express, all because the influencer knows the competition, its offerings, and the direction of the industry as well as anyone inside the company. Better yet, when a popular idea has to go to the cutting-room floor, influencers can explain to upset customers why the idea didn't make it into the product's final version. The influencers can explain the tradeoffs in product development in a way a company never can—and with the authority of a knowledgeable, trusted third party.

Generating Sales

When social media enters the conversation, a lot of marketers talk only about support and launch. They leave post-launch and the rest of the marketing functions to languish and gather mildew under a traditional frame of mind, but even the most mundane or least efficient marketing activities can become more dynamic with just a little creative thinking.

Take a direct mail campaign. It doesn't get much more analog than this: A company sends out a bunch of printed paper and hopes that in return a bunch of potential customers will like what they see. Of course, direct mail takes a little more sophistication than this, but even with that sophistication, only about 5% to 11% of these mailings generate any leads. And if 1% ultimately generates a sale, it often is considered a successful campaign. We realize direct mail has its place when used properly and it's a relatively low-cost way to spark some leads, but social media and word-of-mouth marketing has proven to be far more effective and can actually amplify traditional marketing like direct mail.

Imagine a company that has created an active social-media program with a strong marketing executive who wants to bring proven social-media tools to bear on an entire brand. Looking at the direct-mail campaign shows some new and divergent possibilities. Rather than sending two small mailings to determine the more effective message, the idea comes to float the two sets to some of the influencers and their readers. Further, the company can structure the direct-mail campaign to include third-party endorsements from super-engaged bloggers and other industry experts, and in turn drive potential customers to a Web site where independent customers are saying good things about the company and its products. All this provides the traditional direct campaign with a new level of authority.

What a company says about its own product is all well and good, but customers today want to hear from others with whom they identify (and hence whose opinions they can trust) in order to make an informed buying decision. As proof is the success that HP and our other clients have had with just this type of approach. Traditional marketing is rather uni-dimensional, but add the social-media dimension and the message goes from one-way to two-way or from monologue to dialogue. The same people who inform your market and your customers can help drives leads and convert sales as well as give you ideas for the next product or a greatly improved marketing message—if you properly engage with them.

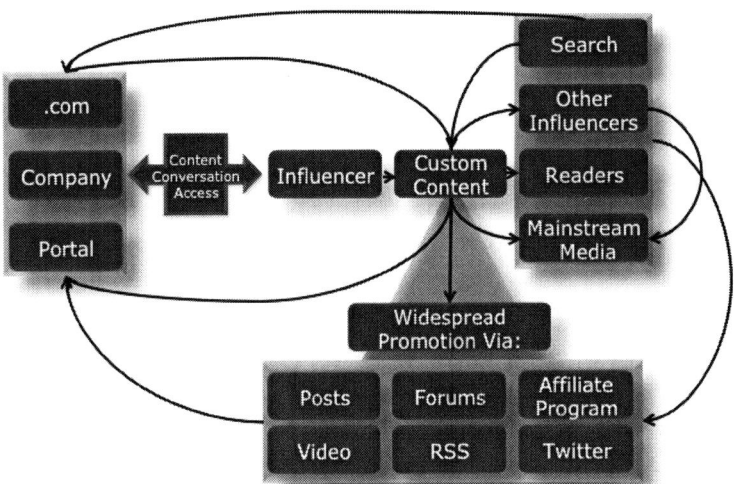

The content flow from the influencers starts in the center and spreads right and down to other venues and media, but brands should also work to leverage this content and move it back to the left by linking to it as a part of their Web, direct, and other traditional marketing efforts.

Service And Support

In the summer of 2007, one of our friends started stocking up for a hike in the US Rockies. He'd hiked on and off for all his life, but after a pause of a couple years, he realized it was high time he resupply himself. Out went all the old gear, clearing the way for a new version of just about all his equipment. He immediately turned to the Internet to start narrowing down his choices.

Now, our friend isn't the easiest person to supply with hiking material. At 6'6", he doesn't fit in the usual sizes for tents or sleeping bags. He had a few brands in mind but needed to know if the newer models would fit. He started searching online forums for information from other tall hikers and eventually found postings on influencer's sites that answered his specific questions. "I never would've believed a 5'9" salesman in a store," he told us. "I needed to hear from someone at least close to my height, and someone who had been out there in the wilderness, who'd actually *been in* that tent or bag." As it turns out, he had a great first hike with the new equipment and even posted an enthusiastic recommendation for the tent he'd been recommended after he and his friends were unexpectedly hit with about four inches of overnight snow.

As our friend will attest, the McKinsey study in Chapter 1 proves that more and more people do, and will, research their products online. More and more people go online to solve their problems, too. Companies that don't integrate social media into their service and support operations risk more hassles, more expenditures, and, frankly, more angry customers. These are lost future sales. For many people, online forums and chatboards have become the "neighbor kid who knows a lot about computers" (or any other product, for that matter). For a growing number of customers, online chat sessions have become a much more comfortable way to interact with an agent than phone queues—and they're cheaper for the companies, to boot.

Take the example of Neowin.net and its tech-support forums. Or consider that Bank of America offers its online banking customers a quick chat session for just about any issue. And many computer vendors now offer a service that allows a technician to take over a customer's PC and fix many problems remotely. These latter two examples are not making use of social media's built-in, outsourced community-support mechanisms that can save companies money and their customers' time. Nothing annoys a customer more than an unanswered question or a problem that lingers and just won't go away. The company that integrates social-media tools across all its functions can find those annoyed customers and relieve their frustration before it turns to anger (and a potential defection to a competitor).

Companies have to make it easy for customers to find the information they need. Search engines are the key, as we all turn to Google (or its competitors) to find the answer we are looking for (which we all know is faster than calling the company for help). Most searches for problems turn up Neowin.net and other similar super-user-driven forums; also, most answers on these sites are far better than the canned FAQs from the company, as forums are written by real people solving real problems just like yours. This double benefit means that customers get better answers faster or understand their problems in more depth when calling company support lines. Either way, it lowers support costs for the company and results in greater satisfaction. Enabling this outsourced support medium for products should be an integral part of a company's judo approach to social media.

Producing Better Messages

The pitches for Microsoft's Windows 7 initially started as just a trickle. Like nearly everyone else on the planet, we knew that Microsoft had the new operating system coming out in late 2009. We got a handful of emails here and there talking about how great it would be, but as the launch date approached, the trickle turned into a full-on flash flood. Marketers across the computing industry began to crank it up in full, and we received at least five emails and two postcards from various tech companies about Windows and how their new products were geared to run it. The PC was going to be fun, fast, and easy again, they promised. Not one of those emails or postcards bothered to say how or why we should upgrade.

For a small business owner or other PC user running Windows XP or Vista and thinking about an upgrade, at no point did Microsoft or its partners provide any truly tangible reason why he or she should make the switch. There was no real impetus for customers to buy unless they already were going to buy anyway, and even then the customers probably would have done a lot of online product research first. Customers know in advance that they can buy from you or from your competitors, so it's vital that you use social media to draw them your way.

We sat there looking at all this information and wondered why none of the companies bothered to include a third-party endorsement. The email, especially, killed us. How hard would it have been to link to one of the PC industry's key influencers and his or her review of the beta version of Windows 7 describing precisely *why* or *how* it was better? Within minutes of thinking on this, we'd listed a dozen ways that social media could've improved this campaign had it been integrated from the start— and this from Microsoft, which has been pretty savvy in harnessing social media in recent years.

We thought, Why not run a social-media campaign that includes a range of ordinary customers upgrading their machines to Windows 7, using it, and talking about the benefits? Microsoft's key online influencers could easily round up some typical customers who'd willingly write reviews for a free copy of the software, and possibly even a new machine. All those emails could have third-party, independent reviews that carry real authority that actually *meant something* to potential buyers. And alongside the email could be easy-to-access "buy here" link. So simple, and so much more effective than the millions of dollars being spent on the actor portrayed in the "Windows 7 Was My Idea" campaign, and yet and opportunity completely overlooked by Microsoft and its partners—all due to them being stuck in a rote pattern of doing the same things in the same ways, despite the current change in their customers' expectations.

Nothing frustrates us more than this; companies so often try to duct tape social media onto their existing programs at the end of the whole marketing-planning process. Everyone sits around the conference table and talks about what they plan to do with all the traditional marketing tools, and with five minutes left in the meeting, they look over at the social-media geek—yes, it's usually a young, mid- or low-level employee. "What do you have in mind?" they ask. This employee says something that the rest don't completely understand; it sure sounds pretty cool, but no one has the time or inclination to discuss it any further. Any chance that they could lower costs and improve the efficacy of their own programs via social media was gone before the meeting even started.

It takes a lot of real work to understand how social media should align with, support, and amplify a company's individual marketing programs. It takes consistent support from the top, including a high-level executive champion who demands that social media penetrates the company's marketing efforts. Until that happens, social media is just another nifty idea from the hipster geek relegated to the end of the meeting.

CHAPTER 5

Kuzushi:
Balance

The focus on balance – *Companies have to go with the flow or get washed away, but knowing how and where to jump in will save them time, energy, and resources.*

WE FIRST MET ROBERT MCLAWS in 2006 at the annual Gnomedex gathering of content producers and technology influencers created by Chris Pirillo. We make it a point to meet a lot of people at conferences. As anyone who has networked around a large conference knows, not all of the random introductions work out very well, so when this 25-year-old, pencil-thin guy walked up to us, asked if we were the guys from AMD, and wondered if he could he pick our brains about social media, we figured, "Here we go again." But if we've learned anything along the way, it's that a good conversation with a blogger is worth its weight in gold. Within minutes, we realized how far off base our initial impression had been. We realized that McLaws concerned himself with the business aspects of computing and how new generations of technology impact business in positive and negative ways. Not much irritated him more than companies that failed to keep abreast of rapid technology changes and left themselves vulnerable to inefficiency or attack. We filed all of that away and promised to stay in touch, glad we hadn't reacted on our first instinct to bolt for the bathroom or come up with some other excuse. We got to know McLaws a little better in the months after that, but it took Microsoft's release of Windows Vista to remind us of how much we had in common with him—and of how mutually beneficial our friendship could become.

The Vista launch wasn't Microsoft's finest moment, and many large enterprises said they wouldn't upgrade from Windows XP. Intel decided not to transition to Vista; AMD opted to make the upgrade. And with that, we figured we could make a point: This represented just one small way in which AMD was striving to take the lead away from Intel in the technological arms race. We got an unenthusiastic (but not altogether unexpected) response from the PR team, so we decided we'd work with some bloggers instead. And because we'd gotten to know him and build a relationship with him, we knew that technological leadership was McLaws' hot button. He'd published several good reviews of Vista and expressed some serious skepticism about all the companies that opted to stick with XP. We figured he'd love this example.

We called him the same day Intel announced it wouldn't make the switch, and soon, we were sarcastically joking about how the US Postal Service would also refuse to upgrade. This evolved into a long rant about how Intel was on the same upgrade cycle as the Postal Service. By the next day, the whole conversation was rewritten and posted on McLaws' blog. McLaws had blasted Intel, praised AMD, and started a wave of positive buzz for AMD across the blogosphere. It's a simple example, but it perfectly illustrates how a good relationship and a conversation with the right content producer can spark a much broader impact than anything we could've produced on our own.

Finding the right time, place, and method to leverage social media is not unlike the judo principle of *kuzushi*. The identification of the right opportunity is central to *kuzushi*, Ohlenkamp explains. For the less experienced, he says, the idea centers on basic physical methods of unbalancing an opponent so one can take control of his or her rival's momentum and use it against the rival, but at a higher level, *kuzushi* becomes a matter of strategy: Knowing when to yield to an opponent's advance allows the fighter to gain control of the contest while maintaining his or her own balance. A judo expert will yield to a greater force, build momentum from it, and, with the proper application of strength at the proper moment, turn the tables to complete the throw. Remember the photo from the previous chapter, which shows that all the movement, and thus all the effort, is in the guy being thrown, not the judo master throwing him? Again, at its purest, the judo throw produces the maximum effect with the minimum effort.

The beauty of word-of-mouth marketing is that it doesn't have to become a Herculean task. A company doesn't need an army of its own bloggers or to spend millions of dollars to generate momentum for itself. Like a master performing a judo throw, a company can tap into the authority and communities of existing key influencers. This is where the results are and leverage the existing flow and generate more buzz from fewer resources. A small company can generate an impact greater than its resources would otherwise allow so in many cases it can compete against larger rivals, and, as we learned in the previous chapter, a big company can amplify its large and sophisticated marketing programs by integrating social media across its operations.

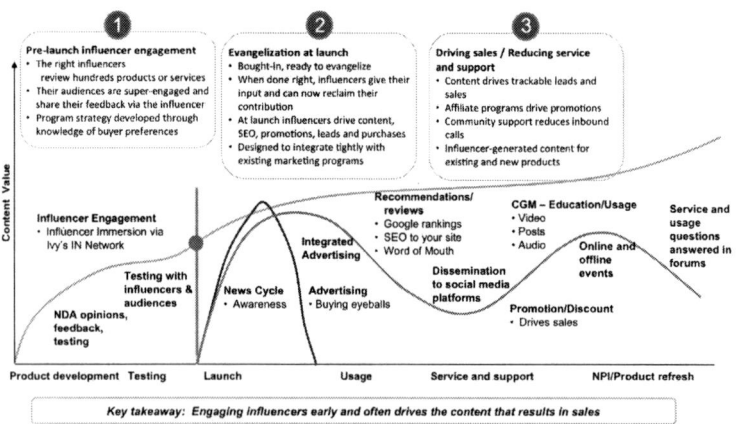

Integrating Judo Social Media across not only the organization but also the brand's or product's lifecycle brings further benefits and drives sales long after launch.

Also like any other marketing channel, however, social media doesn't do the work for you; you have to know in which direction the momentum is headed. Not all social-media approaches fit all marketing programs; you as a marketer need to understand where the momentum and the opportunities are to be successful. They are ubiquitous now, but the Internet and social media, especially, remain young and rapidly changing ecosystems, and the only way to succeed in the midst of all that flux is to have the right mindset, the right relationships, and the willingness to just jump in, engage, and go where the flow takes you. The greatest word-of-mouth marketing ideas will die if a marketer doesn't understand how, where, and when to tap into the blogosphere's existing momentum. The Internet is strewn with all kinds of marketing failures: programs that ignored what influencers needed to build traffic, campaigns that asked bloggers to give from their end but never gave anything back in return, and companies that wasted too much time and energy trying to do everything on their own.

Give Up A Little Control

Budweiser has a long history of brilliant commercials. Very few industries ever found a way to tap into the power of video as well as beer companies did with television ads, so when the production and consumption of consumer-generated video started booming with the advent of YouTube, Blip, Vimeo, and other video sites, it only seemed natural for Budweiser to get in on the action. The company came up with the idea of Bud.tv, an online hub where people would flock to watch clever and funny videos (and of course soak themselves in Budweiser's branding). Budweiser pumped many, many millions of dollars into the project, all while hoping to control what people would talk about and getting them to visit the site.

Consumers have a funny way of deciding what they want to talk about and where they want to go online. Bud.tv didn't attract the millions of visitors that Budweiser's marketing crew envisioned when they launched the channel. The Web's denizens continued to look to YouTube, FunnyOrDie, and

CollegeHumor.com for laughs. For John Moore, an evangelist at WOMMA, Budweiser made the critical mistake of trying to dictate what customers should talk about. "A marketer doesn't decide what gets talked about," Moore says. "People do."

We see many companies try to keep this iron-fisted control over their online marketing campaigns. Rarely, if ever, does it work. With the interaction that's inherent to social media, no marketing message stands a chance of remaining the sole property of the company. Because they can, customers will take the message, add their own two cents, and mold it into something new (and not necessarily something that the company would approve, but, as we've stated, that largely depends on the relationship a company has with its customers). Approach it properly—ceding the customers the control they already have—and a company can sit back and watch as customers take its message, mold it into their own, and give it roots throughout the Internet and with a healthy dose of authority to boot. That's pure gold for a marketing department. Try to retain too much control over the message and you'll be lucky if, like Budweiser, your customers only ignore it.

"Be confident enough in your brand's appeal to say, 'This is what customers are talking about, let's talk about that,'" Moore says. "It goes back to a fundamental truth in business: Businesses must be confident in the products they're bringing to market. They have put their talent, time and money into producing their products or services, bringing the world the ones they feel the most confident about. They can't hope to dictate how people will react, although they can control how the product looks, how it's designed, how it's sourced and built whatever. That might not be the sexy way to go about doing it, but it is certainly the longer-lasting way."

Identify The Right Channel

There are a lot of differing social media approaches and technologies out there. Twitter might be the right platform of choice for some, like cable giant Comcast, which uses it to solve support issues, but this is probably the worst place for a prospective buyer to go to learn about the Comcast, as instead they'll see all of the issues people have with Comcast's cable service. Not a good start for your brand, to say the least. Other companies might gravitate to microsites for quick-turn social endeavors, but these efforts are bankrupt by definition, as they're constructed with limited lifespans in mind. If you or your company suffers from microsite addiction, get help and kick the habit. These properties are *not* truly social, and the world does not need yet another short-term corporate-owned site. In the end, these companies are just wasting money and time that would be far better spent on long-term engagements with influencers who move the needle. Remember, social media judo and all marketing should be about minimum effort and maximum results.

Case in point, Kraft Foods approached us to create a social media campaign for a microsite project they had created around A1 brand steak sauce. They asked us to help create a social-media campaign that would drive traffic to the new microsite. It came up with an "edgy" theme called "Sing for Your Meat," (yes, really) and hoped the microsite would become an online destination where enthusiastic A1 customers could talk or sing about the product by posting videos showing the different ways they love to combine A1 with their meat dishes. That never happened—at least certainly not to the extent that the folks at Kraft hoped it would. We have yet to find a microsite that doesn't serve as a complete and utter social-media dead-end. These properties are one-way roads that ultimately lead customers nowhere, giving nothing of substance to them and providing bloggers no route back into the flow of online traffic. Our friends over at iMedia.com feel the same way and actually wrote an article called "Dead Internet Ideas: Microsites."[6] Get the message?

In the end, A1 managed to generate about 900 comments on their microsite, none of which were illuminating to prospective buyers or that reflected especially well on the brand. For all

[6] See: http://www.imediaconnection.com/content/26857.asp.

the viral-video hits that spill across the Internet, the A1 microsite is bottom of the barrel when it comes to communities who can add anything constructive to the conversation about a brand. And even worse, Kraft had no way of measuring how much impact its efforts had had on A1's sales, as there was no mechanism for driving sales from the microsite (a coupon code, perhaps) and measuring its effect. Kraft had chosen a poor medium for its campaign, but it had also compounded the problem from the start by never really considering how to involve social media and instead confusing customer interaction (however limited) with meaningful customer engagement. Kraft said to us, "We've built this microsite, and now we want you to bolt on a social-media campaign and drive traffic to it." They'd picked the wrong medium and wrong approach. Worse yet, they went forward with their hand out, expecting something to be given to them without offering anything in return.

Here is a quick snapshot of what might have made this program much more successful and going in the right direction: We would have suggested recruiting somewhere in the neighborhood of 20 to 25 influential bloggers to serve as judges of "Sing for Your Meat" contest entries. Ideally, these influencers would be brought to Kraft HQ outside Chicago in advance of the campaign's launch, and judging would take place as part of an "A1 Day" at the Kraft kitchens. The influencers would not only judge contest entries but also be given a tour of Kraft's test kitchens and meet with A1 employees to have ample material for generating content such as blog posts, tweets, videos, and podcasts. Further, we thought the content would be generated via influencers' engagement with their audiences before, during, and after the tour of Kraft HQ and judging of entries. Add to this content a limited-time offer such as a unique discount coupon or incentive to sign up for direct emails from Kraft and they'd have a measureable promotional effort that could significantly impact sales.

What would this have yielded for Kraft and A1, as well as for the influencers? Let's break it down:

- By leveraging influencer presence at Kraft HQ and also in the judging, Kraft would have gained a much greater reach for its campaign, and this would have been combined with third-party endorsement. The influencers' promotion of A1, the contest, and Kraft in general via multiple social media channels would have driven awareness and sales.

- Influencers would gain both access and credibility via direct interaction with Kraft staff, while also generating a load of unique and differentiated content for their sites.

To complement the direct participation of first-stage influencers, we could have recruited a second group of around 20 more influencers to work with the first, all of whom would be eligible give away A1-branded gifts or other sales promotions. Additionally, Kraft could bring the winning contestants and the judges to Chicago for a real-world event, perhaps renting part of the Wrigley Field parking lot during a Chicago Cubs game, where the winners and judges would prepare their own special recipes for the crowd, engaging them in casual yet meaningful conversation about cooking with A1. They could have also passed out coupons or other coded promotional items and tracked those items' subsequent impact on sales. These second-stage activities would be designed to assist influencers in generating yet more A1-specific content, extending the reach and life of the "Sing for Your Meat" campaign over a sustained multi-week period. This would create a minor media event, thus propagating influencer content via other sites as well as mainstream media. And it would drive sales via yet more credible third-party endorsement in the process.

This second stage would also have benefits:

- Kraft would gain publication and propagation of additional consumer-generated content that would further boost overall audience participation and add potential for

Chris Aarons, Geoff Nelson and Nick White with Dan Zehr

viral pass-through. And let's not forget additional measureable sales gains.

- Influencers would produce more content, gaining traffic
and additional credibility via further evidence of their
close-knit relationships with the major brand, Kraft.

Take all this into account and you're likely to see how identifying and inserting a judo move into even this campaign, well after
it was baked, would have vastly boosted its impact to brand awareness and sales gains. What's more, we didn't suggest a radical
departure from the initial plan, as the writing was on the wall that
Kraft was not open to reconsidering the "Sing for Your Meat"
campaign, so, although our proposal would not have dramatically
changed the course of the campaign, we'd bet heavily that it would
have contributed much better overall results—while making a
hero of some farsighted marketing manager in the process.

A Shared Message

Someday in the future, our kids or yours will work for
someone like Chris Lesinski of Hackcollege.com. We worked
with Lesinski on the Party-in-a-Box campaign discussed in
Chapter 2, and in so doing, we quickly realized that he sees
social media and marketing in ways that few other people do. It
therefore came as no surprise that he got straight to the core of
the issue recently when we discussed how companies should
think about their marketing messages once they set the messages loose in the blogosphere and beyond. Let us give you
some detail as to what we're driving at here.

A marketing program's content and distribution can't exist
as two distinct functions in a social-media environment, Lesinski says. This statement struck us as sort of a Marshall
McLuhan "the medium is the message" moment, when the
message becomes defined in part by the social-media channels
through which it flows. This is largely because the message
itself changes as it passes from person to person, having been

filtered and interpreted by each individual who consumes it. Though in traditional marketing channels each person could interpret the brand message in different ways, the opportunity to rebroadcast his or her interpretation to the world hasn't always existed. The advent of social media allows for this very phenomenon, so the message now inevitably becomes as much the customer's as it does the company's. Lesinski, who has worked with Comedy Central and the *Los Angeles Times*, expresses this in newspaper terms (relating it to a decidedly "old" medium that everyone can understand): "When newspapers started having Web sites, they were ancillary to journalists' workflow. They just threw their news onto their Web site, without changing the articles in any substantial fashion" he says. "Then they realized the need to integrate the Web site and the print product, so that the two sides were working together. Right now, marketing companies are making a similar mistake, in that they are used to having both a broadcast guy and a theatrical guy – but there needs to be a different approach, where it's more holistic. They need to reexamine the workflow."

We couldn't agree more. Word-of-mouth marketing has raised questions about whether a company should consider social media in the context of its marketing content or as just another avenue for its marketing message. Those of you reading this far should have no doubt by now that we firmly believe in the former. As Lesinski notes, however, this remains a weird line that no one has drawn yet. At Comedy Central, he says, social media is a more integrated part of the whole marketing function, so any content creation automatically takes social media into account, yet most newspapers have taken a more tortuous route, where the once hard-and-fast separation between content and business has morphed into a much closer relationship. "At the L.A. Times, where I've been involved, their social media guy worked with content," Lesinski says. "That strikes me as strange. He was kind of 'marketing' the content. It seemed so weird in a journalism aspect, having someone responsible for marketing but also working in the content, non-business side."

Journalism represents its own unique case, of course, but it also serves to illustrate how inseparable the creation and distribution of the marketing message has become. And as Lesinski notes, this change will force marketing departments wanting to employ social media programs to realize two interlinked truths: (1) Customers will take your message and make it their own and (2) You have to plan accordingly as a result. "I don't think a company can blindly throw a product out there anymore and just let it morph on its own, especially online, where you have such a large amount of people out there," he says. "There's a mob mentality; people will start running in a particular direction of their own volition, even if it's not an accurate way to perceive a product. For companies to start with some sort of an idea of how to direct this, is helpful." In fact, we'd go further and say it's *vital*.

But what then? What happens if the message starts careening off point? This is a clear danger for companies who play in the blogosphere, but taking the right mindset of truly collaborating with key influencers will dramatically reduce the chances of it happening. "I have no idea how a company can subtly massage the discussion in their favor" once online communities have taken possession and control of it, Lesinski says. "There might not be a way to do it. It might not even be worth doing. But I don't think there's anything wrong with a company defending itself when there are legitimate reasons behind it."

And here's the one point at which we differ, albeit only slightly, with Lesinski. A company might not have much chance to sway discussions once they start blazing across the blogosphere—at least not if that wayward discussion has merit to it. Nevertheless, by working collaboratively with key influencers and approaching social media with a willingness to share your brand message with your customers—a willingness born out of confidence in your company and your products—you create the potential to shift any unintended consequences in your favor.

The Wal-Mart Moms

We couldn't go through this chapter without mentioning Wal-Mart's "Elevenmoms." Quite frankly, we have a lukewarm opinion of the world's largest retailer on the whole, but we have to give the company credit for finding a pitch-perfect group of influencers for its brand. The company has identified a group of 11 women who represent the core message of the Wal-Mart brand: saving money. Each influencer blogs about her life experiences with a bent toward saving—anything from recipes to dealing with kids to balancing work and home. The members have blogs such as FrugalUpstate.com and DealSeeking-Mom.com. On occasion, they drop in links to Wal-Mart promotions or talk about ways the retailer plays into their day-to-day existence.

"Mommy" bloggers (a term that's not universally loved by them but that's universally understood by all) are a different breed of blogger, and Wal-Mart chose its group very wisely. It took advantage of these bloggers' ability to influence like-minded shoppers. Wal-Mart's Elevenmoms beautifully illustrate how a company that identifies the right influencers can leverage social media to beneficially spread its brand and message.

Few companies can dictate terms to their key influencers in the same manner Wal-Mart can—customers have a funny way of demanding what they want, especially online, where they can voice their opinions both freely and constantly—but even the Wal-Mart example shows that a successful word-of-mouth marketing program has to work in concert with key influencers. Ultimately, if you scratch their backs, they'll scratch yours.

We'll say it again, however: None of this really takes flight until a company adopts a truly social and giving mindset. Only then do key influencers become willing guides and partners through the social-media jungle. Only then will the content producers begin to offer their invaluable advice for improving your products, services, and online marketing efforts. And only then will they give you the benefit of the doubt when something inevitably goes awry. They've built their audiences by understanding what works and what doesn't, and they will share their expertise with a company that consistently shows that it's willing to give them something in return.

One old cliché doesn't hold true; familiarity breeds respect, not contempt, in the case of online influencers. The company that respects its customers and influencers will quickly realize it can loosen its iron-fisted grip on every little detail of its brand message and the delivery of it. It can plan and execute a marketing campaign that goes with the flow of the online community, not against it, and avoids drifting off course into places unwanted or unknown. This company will leverage social media's existing momentum to save its time, energy, and resources, and when that begins to happen—when a company has a frank and free-flowing relationship with online influencers that benefits all participants—the company will consistently get back as much as it gives.

CHAPTER 6

Randori:
Free Practice

PERSONAL-COMPUTER MAKERS LOVE THE well-educated high-power user. In a world of fluctuating PC sales volumes and steadily declining margins, the people who need masses of computer power from their desktops or notebooks offer PC manufacturers one of the few available opportunities to reliably fatten profits. And if those power users happen to work in cool and creative jobs, all the better. The brand halo vastly helps overall image, and vice versa. Look at Apple, which dominates sales of high-end computers to many of the top creative industries, including graphic design, filmmaking, and photography. Granted, much of Apple's popularity stems from its design, ease of use, and ubiquity of the iPhone, iPad and other products, but make no mistake, the buzz factor generated by high-demand, high-end creative types still plays a significant role, and every computer maker very much covets attention of that sort.

HP wanted to tap into this halo effect with the launch of its Envy line of PCs. In 2006, the company acquired Voodoo Computers, an edgy boutique PC maker that had an ardent following amongst game players. HP eventually wrapped the design and expertise underpinning Voodoo's high-end gaming rigs into the Envy line. With low-cost netbooks rapidly accelerating the decline in average PC sales prices, HP hoped the decision to incorporate Voodoo's extra-creative DNA into Envy would help it make inroads to the more-profitable higher end of the market. This was a classic anti-commoditization strategy, and the thought behind it was well-founded, so HP designed a set of sleek, minimalistic, high-powered computers that were loaded with all the bells and whistles a super-user would expect, although not cluttered by them. When it came time to launch the new Envy notebooks, HP knew it would have to somehow venture into Apple territory: It would have to get the Envy in front of creative types.

HP came to us for help, as we were the one agency that consistently drove revenues and brand image for them time and again. Honestly, the basis for our plan to help launch Envy was derived straight from our earlier success with Party-in-a-Box. As you remember, that program's success came about by our working with top college bloggers to create an event where hundreds of their peers could play around with HP's Windows Vista-powered dv2 notebook. And as we mentioned in previous chapters, Party-in-a-Box managed to generate *a lot* of buzz for HP's dv2, accompanied by a huge boost in traffic for the bloggers and, ultimately, a significant jump in sales of the dv2—all of this on the cusp of Microsoft's launch of Windows 7. In light of what we'd accomplished, we figured, why shouldn't the same basic approach work to introduce the Envy to the professional and semi-professional creative crowd? So we set out to modify Party-in-a-Box in ways that would connect online demand generation with a unique, credible, and hands-on real-world experience.

What resulted was a series of events, all developed and executed by bloggers influential in the digital creative space, each of which put the Envy notebook into the hands of creative professionals and semi-professionals—the people who will willingly and without hesitation spend thousands of dollars on the right gear for their creative pursuits. Hence, they were the right audience to whom to pitch a higher-end PC offering that would support their creative aspirations. What's more, the programming of the events was unique and distinctly appealing to this type of creative-minded individual, presenting the Envy line of PC s in a context that absolutely made sense to them.

This is important, because if we'd merely adapted Party-in-a-Box and slapped the model onto Envy, the designers would have had the opportunity to interact with the product, but not in a way that really mattered to them—the original Party-in-a-Box event model would have been too constraining and not engaging in the right ways. Instead, because these creative folks want their computers to quickly render huge graphical or musical chores and display them in super-sharp detail, we did what's always worked for us in the past: gave the influential bloggers a free hand in programming their events to meet the exact needs and expectations of the attendees. After all, the bloggers' own brands were also intrinsically linked to the events they were creating, so the success or failure of each event would have a direct and immediate bearing on the blogger's own standing.

As it happened, then, we put together a comprehensive social media plan that partnered Envy with influential creative bloggers who would execute a series of real-world events in 10 major US cities, covering a range of creative arts, from music production to photography to filmmaking. The events did not focus on the Envy at their core, but rather integrated the machines into the event flow itself, letting people interact with the notebooks (or not) in a natural way and completely at their leisure. The events weren't fundamentally about the Envy PC, but they did allow these highly sought-after high-power users to see and use the computer in a context that made complete sense to them as creative content producers.

By way of example, one of the site owners we worked with put together a pretty chic event in Santa Monica with the National Association of Television Production Executives, thanks to a blogger who was part of this organization. The event featured a panel discussion on the future of digital media, with the exchange centering on the emergence of new, more-powerful mainstream technologies offering enough horsepower to replace some of the more expensive proprietary systems that digital content producers had come to use in the past. Creative content producers and industry executives could play around with the Envy to see how it compared with some of their current systems, from the vantage point of keeping up with the latest advances in digital creative technology.

Of course, no other event had this same format, each one being very different from the next, and each focusing on a particular digital creative industry or profession; nevertheless, in each case, we'd identified people who were likely to be predisposed to HP's message and invited them to assemble their peers in places where they'd be immediately comfortable and thus more likely to embrace the Envy message. In other words, we helped influential bloggers put the Envy in a context where creative professionals and enthusiasts would be entertained, enlightened, or both, then we provided the professionals and enthusiasts an opportunity to interact with the product in a way that suited their natural inclinations. And don't forget, we helped significantly enhance the sponsoring bloggers' images and traffic stats in the process.

All told, we ran 10 of these events for less than the price of a quarter-page ad in most magazines. We arranged to have Envy PCs at each event, and we worked with relevant bloggers to figure out how to build each event and incorporate a giveaway that would energize the target audience. In doing so, HP built credibility within a valuable market and also buzz, largely because each influential blogger would of course promote the heck out of his or her own event. Meanwhile, the blogger's stature in his or her niche—and the blogger's online traffic— would jump (dramatically, in many cases). If we already knew someone whose site addressed one of the target markets, we'd plug them in.

Our friend Xavier Lanier, who runs Notebooks.com, is an avid photographer. He's the sort of guy who has several thousands of dollars of photography equipment and actually knows how to use each piece to its fullest extent. Lanier is part of a photography club in San Francisco. The group gets together regularly to talk shop and to experiment with new, often difficult, challenges so as to further their expertise. He thought that involving his photography group would be a great way to get the Envy in front of advanced photographers with fairly deep pockets. We couldn't have agreed more.

Thus, Lanier got the group together one evening at Dolores Park in the city. They hired a fire-dance troupe to come by, with the group seeking to practice ways to capture excellent pictures of an interesting subject in what turned out to be rather difficult lighting conditions (late evening). After a couple hours of shooting, the club departed for a rooftop bar Lanier had rented for the evening. There, they could pull out their camera memory cards, load the photos onto the Envy PCs, and discuss each other's pictures, picking out the best ones by majority vote. At the end of the night, the club member with the best photo was awarded the Envy PC to take home and apply to the craft.

Ultimately, these events promoting HP's Envy line became the bloggers' pet projects. With a fair amount of direction and an Envy PC, we let them run away with the projects. Of course, we had to be smart about the bloggers we brought into the project, and we also had to discuss their ideas and execution plans well in advance—it simply wouldn't have worked to bring in an Apple zealot, of course. But after that, we knew we shouldn't— and even couldn't—control their actions, at the very least because we were not experts in the digital media space and didn't know what would appeal most to attendees. We could guide things at the outset to bring about the results HP desired, but ultimately we and HP had to give up control and go with the flow. Far too many companies get in their own way, feeling like they need to control the message at every step. When it comes to social media, however, the corporate marketing department has only one vote; to accomplish anything, it has to collaborate with its customers and industry influencers, who have their own seats at the table and, in many ways, have more power and sway over the perceptions that will, or will not, bring about the outcomes our clients want.

The different Envy events never amassed the traffic that 31 Days of the Dragon did, but it didn't matter. The target for the

Envy events was a smaller and higher-value group of users—a more closed circle. The events didn't have to—and weren't designed to—cross into the mainstream consumer consciousness. Most people aren't in the market for a machine like HP's Envy, and if they saw it, they would not contemplate spending what it costs; nevertheless, the Envy campaign worked precisely the way we'd hoped: It went viral within the circles of the specific high-power, high-value users who matter for that style of notebook PC. Plus, it drove sales, which, according to HP, is all that really matters in the end.

A Little Bit Of Magic

The success of the Envy campaign relied on our ability to find the right influencers, and that's not always easy in the volatile, mixed-up online world. A person who might make a perfect pitch for one product might not make a great influencer for another. As we learned with the Envy, certain digital video or photography bloggers would work much better than the technology-focused influencers we'd typically dealt with in programs past. Marketers who are adept at parsing out the best influencers, not just relevant or related content producers, are taking the step from acceptable results to truly remarkable results that move the business forward.

In judo, the bridge from novice to expert passes through *randori*, or free practice. It's a fitting term for the vortex where online and offline marketing meet, too. *Ran* means chaos, and *dori* means hold. In judo, *randori* refers to the way a fighter manages the unexpected, and the unexpected always arises during practice or a match. In marketing, the idea of *randori* relates to the way a company must focus its marketing efforts to incorporate the best influencers and forums—both online and in the real world—*before they're needed*. It means building relationships first and foremost, then working with those influencers to identify the right sites (online) and events (offline) through which to disseminate your message.

As we discussed in previous chapters, no social-media marketing campaign should stand on its own. Online and real-world word-of-mouth efforts should serve as a low-cost way to improve a company's entire marketing portfolio, not to replace it or to perform as a mere sideshow. We've found that, on average, about 60% of what we do amplifies traditional marketing endeavors. The remaining 40% operates within the realm of word-of-mouth marketing itself. A company cannot deceive itself into thinking that social media activity for its own sake will work to the fullest potential. Similarly, no social media program can live alone in the virtual world. Marketers have to apply the benefit of word-of-mouth marketing to all its other marketing pursuits, such as product design, sales training, and post-purchase support. They also must find ways to graft online marketing with a real-life event or experience. Doing this might be as simple as conducting a product giveaway— one lucky dog wins an honest-to-goodness product—or it might involve holding seminars and other events, such as Party-in-a-Box or the influencer-led events programs in promotion of the HP Envy. When the idea strikes an especially emotional chord with the target customers while simultaneously offering them a tangible, real-life benefit, well, then you can create a little magic.

Jason Dunn, the Canadian blogger introduced in Chapter 2, sparked just such an idea. The economy had started to really tank toward the end of 2008, the headlines perpetually screaming of company failures and broad-reaching layoffs. The cuts hit some industries harder than others and certainly didn't spare technology workers, many of whom suddenly found themselves looking for work. Some opted to start new businesses or to volunteer to keep busy, and others didn't have the means to buy PCs for their kids to keep up with schoolwork. Dunn suggested a program that would help influential bloggers help their readers over the holiday season, whether those readers recently laid off or otherwise facing a downward turn in circumstances. This was the genesis of the HP Magic Giveaway.

First, let us provide a little background to those of you who don't deal with technology influencers regularly. Suffice it to say, these content producers receive *tons* of equipment to review, and at some point they have to decide what to do with all this stuff. In many cases, the company asks the influencers to return the review unit. In others, the company lets the influencer keep the product or give it away—a little bonus for readers, and one that doesn't hurt a content producer's online traffic, either. Either way, as we learned with the Vista launch discussed earlier, the influencers have to disclose where the product comes from and what they're doing with it over the long haul.

The HP Magic campaign would generously provide review units of 7 products (valued at $6000 in total) to 50 top bloggers across technology, gaming, mobile, college-aged, Hispanic, female-centric, and other market categories, and each of the participating influencers was asked to give away those machines after reviewing them. With HP's help, we managed to add some special elements that really made this campaign take off. First, HP and Microsoft supplied a boatload of products—more than $6,000 worth—*to each influencer.* The package included an HP TouchSmart PC, three HP notebooks, an HP printer, and an assortment of other products. Second, and more important in the long run, we took Dunn's suggestion and encouraged every influencer to incorporate some sort of charitable element in his or her program. There were no hard-and-fast rules. We suggested that influencers give the whole package away and ask the winners to carve off a portion to donate it to someone (or some organization).

Shane Pitman, who was still at Neowin.net at the time, set up a contest and awarded the products as prizes to people who could make the site's logo "out of real life elements and make it look as magical as possible. You could make the logo out of bananas, chairs or anything you can get your hands on. Be as creative as possible and take a picture of the finished product." He and his colleagues didn't include the TouchSmart PC in the prize package, instead choosing to provide it to a children's hospice in the spirit of the contest.

Other influencers asked readers to describe how they would spread the holiday cheer if they won. At Notebooks.com, Xavier

Lanier and his colleagues designed the contest in a way that awarded points for different social-media activities, such as sharing content from the site through Facebook or Twitter. The greatest number of points went to people who described how they would donate some or all of the prize package to charity and how it would be put to good use as a result. In Lanier's case, "The winner ended up giving it away to a local children's hospital. He was able to give it in the name of our community site and also in his own name. He kept just one computer. So it's beyond just our giving a prize. Now you have a community that says, 'We didn't win the Note-books.com contest, but we still got something good out of it.'"

The influencers designed and executed the whole program, and they were smart about how they did it. Just like before and the way we advise our clients, we told the bloggers, "Give it away any way you'd like." Most of them left it up to their communities to decide the most worthy causes. Readers provided the second level of the award (i.e., describing how they'd share their winnings), and consequently freed the bloggers from pre-scribing anything to their communities. This never would've worked had we scripted a single approach for all of the 50 different influencers, and likewise, it wouldn't have generated nearly as much buzz if the influencers had scripted the giveaways for their communi-ties. We instead opted to get the snowball rolling downhill and let it grow of its own accord from there. After the first few influencers posted their contests, displaying an astonishing degree of creativity in the process, the rest jumped on board, and the ingenuity continued as the contest progressed—and it went viral for all the right reasons. The influencers got something out of it. Their communities got some-thing out of it. People who were hurting through capricious circum-stance got something out of it—even from people they didn't know. Everyone felt good about helping their fellow human beings.

Also, lest we forget, HP and Microsoft were on the receiving end of a positive wave of buzz, plus a boost in sales during the critical hol-iday season. The campaign generated 980,000 Google links, and more than 65 million people viewed it online.[7] Traffic for the bloggers increased 40% on average. Sales and branding improved for HP and

---

[7] According to data from Alexa.com.

Microsoft during the very important holiday season. Once again, there were benefits for all.

Online Marketing Is Not PR

As you've seen by now, we worked with HP and Microsoft on most of our highest-profile campaigns. Those two companies have displayed some of the most progressive thinking to date when it comes to social-media marketing, but both are huge companies, and each has to deal with the constant upheaval endemic to an organization of that size. At HP, we've found that some groups understand our approach to social media better than others. That's to be expected in a large company in the Fortune 50. At Microsoft, an organizational change has turned its Windows group, among others, from one of the leaders in social media into a source of frustration for many of the bloggers with whom we work.

The jury is still out on what sort of mindset Microsoft will take toward social media and word-of-mouth marketing, but when we asked the influencers we know about their biggest pet peeves, Microsoft kept popping up. The company, which has made great inroads with bloggers over the past decade, apparently has lost its way by the beginning of 2010. Many key influencers weren't happy with the way the company is currently handling relationships with them.

Initially, the company collaborated with the bloggers regularly, working hard to include them in events and product milestones, keeping them informed of upcoming projects, and generally leaning on their expertise to expose new ideas and opportunities. There was a definite preference being demonstrated to their influencer core, and Microsoft's online efforts flourished for it for quite some time. More recently, influencers say, the company has closed them off, and its management of social media has come from more of a PR sort of orientation. We spend much of our time studying different approaches to social media campaigns, and we have yet to see a PR department or firm run a truly successful word-of-mouth campaign that capitalizes on every advantage it presents. Successful word-of-mouth marketing absolutely has to encompass the entire marketing department and the entire product cycle. The PR department contributes an important piece to that, but it's only just a piece.

The bigger problem, though, is the democratization of the product message and brand ownership, a process that runs counter to the traditional PR mindset. The art of public relations seeks to control the message, or at least control its cadence and tenor, as well as the medium in which it's conveyed. Apologies for bursting that bubble, but those of us who work regularly with social media influencers saw that horse leave the barn years ago. Customers and influencers now are co-owners of a brand—irrevocably so. These days, someone in Timbuktu can take your product and feature it in a high-definition video that draws millions of viewers from all over the globe. In turn, those millions of viewers can post their own opinions, reviews, and videos about the product. You're delusional if you think a corporate blog, your company Web site, or a neutered press release that manages to spawn a pair of newspaper articles will influence more opinions than those millions of like-minded people online. Someone acting as a third party will, by definition, have more credibility than any self-promoting company can ever hope to have. If that third party cares about your product, it will play a role in setting the tone for the product's reception in the marketplace, whether that tone is good or bad. Why not dispense with the illusion, come to this realization, and collaborate with them?

To work with influential bloggers, you have to build a two-way relationship. These customers aren't just an audience, they're players on the social-media stage as well, and frankly, they are much better at social media than most companies. Whether or not you want them to, they're going to take your script and make it their own. Far too often, PR departments want to control the outbound message, to whom it goes, and what it says, but their oversight here is not just missing the democratization of the brand and brand message; controlling the message actually works counter to meeting a customer's needs. Today, companies must view influencers as participants—true stakeholders, not just verbal candy that companies throw around at annual meetings. The companies that don't include customers and influencers in their marketing processes run the risk of losing all control of their message in the end, no matter the caliber of their traditional PR departments.

A Personal Touch

The ironic thing about all this is that the further a company pushes its marketing into the virtual world, the more actual relationships it needs to build. Online word-of-mouth marketing can deliver tremendous efficiency in terms of scale and scope, but it still requires a personal connection and an ongoing interaction with the gatekeepers to those audiences.

Johan van Mierlo, who writes for MobilityMinded.com, shared one such cautionary tale on our Ivy Worldwide internal forums. A couple public relations firms wanted to make their interactions with online influencers more efficient, van Mierlo said, so they pitched a program that would have required influencers to regularly check in with them via their online systems when seeking information and contacts. The resulting "relationship" would live almost entirely on the Internet. Very much to their credit, the PR agencies consulted with online content producers before going live with the idea, and, based on the negative feedback, decided to put the project on hold. "Times have changed," van Mierlo said, "and I think we need to have access to the executives and the PR people both in person and online. Just online will be a loss, and just over the phone is a loss." The same critical balance of online and offline interaction holds true when connecting with customers. Companies can't—and shouldn't—resist the low cost and broad reach that the Internet brings to online marketing campaigns, but no one has found a virtual way to re-create the full impact of a direct, in-person, real-life interaction with a company's people or products. Chances are, no one ever will—the Internet can replace only so much of the physical world.

This leaves marketing professionals with a new challenge. They have to find the right blend of authentic, in-person experiences—what is called "experiential marketing" these days— and combine this with the reach and flexibility of online word-of-mouth campaigns. Although the Internet gives a company the scale to vastly broaden its reach and massively reduce its cost per touch, customers remain much more likely to buy after a real-life experience, and although a positive in-person experience more often leads to a sale, a company can't get the whole world in one place at one time. Many things that a marketer can't do online, can be done offline, and vice versa. That's why connecting the online marketing campaign with a real-world corollary works so well, and it's why many companies are scrambling to better understand the give-and-take between the two.

The one common denominator in all of this remains the personal relationship. In experiential marketing, a company tries to create a personal relationship between its brand and its customer. In marketing through social media, we create personal relationships with the influencers, who in turn serve as gatekeepers to the millions of people we want to reach but don't have the resources to contact on our own. We leverage the scale they provide us, but only because they trust us enough to let us. And gaining that trust requires a social mindset and a personal relationship.

The PR firms that van Mierlo told us about earlier didn't have a terrible idea. They simply had lost sight of the most important fundamental step in the process: establishing and nurturing the relationship on a personal level. Marketing through social media won't allow companies to abandon personal contact with influencers any more than they can abandon personal contact with their customers—after all, influencers are customers, too—instead, marketing via social media simply allows a company to leverage the right personal relationships and to work with those influential voices to reach an audience it never could, or never could afford to, reach before. Only after a company commits to an ongoing relationship can it supplement its social-media marketing efforts with the various kinds of virtual forums, sounding boards, and information-sharing tools.

We've come up with a few simple techniques that simply help influencers accomplish their goals in one way or another. None of the techniques are especially unique, but by putting them together, we've created an anytime, everyday way to keep open the communication channels when Ivy Worldwide and the influencers with whom we work can't see one another face to face.. For example, we run the Influential Network, an array of forums where influencers can engage in a range of discussions and share thoughts on the good, the bad, and the ugly with us, our clients and each other. Many of the ideas for this book came directly out of that forum, including the example van Mierlo mentioned. We also have a service we call Ivy Media, which we use to aggregate online advertising placements and supply them to member sites. After all, there's no real-world connection with influencers quite like helping them earn cold, hard cash. Ivy Media is not something we pulled out of the ether; other firms have set up similar networks. Those ideas all work, and work well (not as well as ours, we've been told), but to capitalize on the full potential these influencers offer, we have to create that real-world, real-person relationship first. That's what makes our programs sing.

The Right Partners

In some cases, developing the right relationships is the only reason a campaign works. Clearly, we work most often with technology bloggers, as we founded Ivy Worldwide coming from technology backgrounds, but when HP came to us to help build some buzz for a collaboration with the National Basketball Association, we realized the idea had nothing novel for the usual tech bloggers with whom we worked.

The HP–NBA combination isn't a natural one to begin with, so we had to work hard to bring the right audiences together. We turned to an array of sports bloggers, in particular the network of writers who post to BleacherReport.com, a popular sports site with contributors in most major cities. In doing so, we had to stretch a bit and move beyond our technology comfort zone to approach a new set of bloggers, but, as expected, the same principles we'd applied in our earlier work apply universally to influencers of other stripes. Despite the awkward combination of brands, we still managed to find a way to help bloggers build their audiences while promoting our clients' interests in the process. With the help of the NBA, we lined up several well-known retired basketball stars in major cities, including Dominique Wilkins in Atlanta and Kareem Abdul-Jabbar in Los Angeles. They would drop by a local Best Buy to sign autographs and take photos, all of which was coordinated using HP products. Of course, we'd have a bunch of HP computers and printers displayed there as well. People could use the HP printers in display to print hardcopies of the photos they took with the NBA stars, so we had a decent and practical demonstration of the technology—and one that made sense in the moment.

Admittedly, this wasn't a really graceful transition from the NBA to HP, or vice versa, yet the principles underlying our approach were still the very same ones we'd successfully employed in dozens of past programs. We sought out bloggers who had a certain level of influence in this particular community (e.g., the NBA), and we extended to them an opportunity they would appreciate and that, hopefully, would help build their audiences at the same time. We brought the sports bloggers into the planning of the events and made sure they got some one-on-one time with the Hall of Famer before the public descended upon him. Given such an opportunity, the bloggers relentlessly promoted the events, and with their exclusive access, they produced exclusive content for their sites. This content was syndicated to nonparticipating sites and the mainstream media as well, thus vastly increasing message penetration. The HP–NBA combination didn't make for the perfect campaign by any stretch of the imagination, but our fundamental social mindset allowed us to take an awkward combination of brands and pull off a series of events that were successful in the eyes of both our clients and these influential sports bloggers. By extending ourselves first, then asking the influencers how they could help us in return, we managed to turn a head-scratcher of a strategic partnership into a whole series of successful events.

The moral of the story is that some campaigns just come together perfectly and some take a lot more effort and planning. Sometimes, the outcome simply can't be fully known ahead of time, and the discovery process is the part of the campaign's goals. If marketing was all science and no art, we wouldn't need creatives and could rely solely on reams of research. The very fact that you're dealing with human beings mean you have to morph and blend and adjust along the way, and the campaign becomes a sort of science experiment whose purpose, in part, is to find out what's going to happen in the end. You must stick to your principles and objectives, clearly, but you also have to cede a measure of control to the experiment itself to get the full effect. Regardless, starting with a social mindset and building relationships with the right influencers is the only way to bring out the full value of social media. With those fundamentals in place, online marketing begins to execute itself. Define the strategy, float the idea, refine it with influencer input, and launch it. Then, iterate with the influencers in your camp to continually adapt and guide the campaign where it needs to go to meet your aims. After all of that, enjoy what happens to your sales, your brand, and your share.

CHAPTER 7

Shiai:
Contest

DO YOU REMEMBER THE ELF Yourself campaign? We ask the question at almost every presentation, training, or college class we teach, and most people remember the campaign immediately. The fad swept the Web in late 2006 and lasted through the next several holiday shopping seasons. Someone could upload a photo and paste his or her face (or just as likely, a friend's face) onto the body of an entourage of dancing, singing elves. Then, of course, the person emailed it out to everyone they knew. It was a surefire viral hit for ... well, what company was it for? We ask that question, too. Most people know the campaign very well and have even participated, but few can name the brand.

The Elf Yourself campaign quickly became the darling of the advertising world. Magazines wrote glowing articles about it. Media bloggers broke it down and debated the underlying reasons for its widespread appeal and viral success. Every company wanted a program the likes of Elf Yourself, and why not? According to a report in *Advertising Age*, 26.4 million people spent the equivalent of 2,600 years at the Elf Yourself page during its initial launch. At the height of the 2008 holiday season, 10 people would "elf themselves" each second. Numerous mainstream media outlets including ABC's Good Morning America, VH1, and countless others ran stories about the campaign.

Now, again, what company was behind that campaign? The success of Elf Yourself should've put the company's name on everyone's lips, yet the company's sites got virtually no boost in the Google search rankings, in large part because the campaign spread almost exclusively through email and instant messaging. Although almost 30,000 Web sites had linked to ElfYourself.com, the page that managed to generate all that user affection was linked to just one other site: OfficeMax.com. Oh yeah, *Office Max*, the company behind the whole Elf Yourself phenomenon. Office Max saw no real boost to its sales after unleashing one of the most viral campaigns in Web history—Office Max, the company whose vice president, Bob Thacker, told *Advertising Age*, "We were looking to build the brand, warm up our image. *We weren't looking for sales.* We are third-place players in our industry, so we are trying to differentiate ourselves through humor and humanization" [emphasis added].

Office Max's Elf Yourself campaign.

Office Max failed on all accounts, including its attempts to "warm up [its] image." We asked thousands of people if they knew which company did Elf Yourself, and those who had any answer almost always said Office Depot or Staples. *The overwhelming majority of customers who saw Office Max's popular marketing campaign gave credit to the company's top competitors!* Talk about an epic marketing failure. The US is home to three big-box office supply retail chains. One of them runs one of the most successful viral campaigns in the history of mankind, yet its competitors get credit for it and retain —perhaps even bolster— their own greater brand recognition. There ought to be an award for this level of underachievement. We wrote this book to show how companies can do more with less by harnessing the power of social media, word of mouth, and online communities. Elf Yourself is the absolute pinnacle, the hallmark, the reigning world champion of the exact opposite; it's the antithesis of judo marketing. You can make all the right moves, spend tons of money, and create a massive wave of buzz, but it means absolutely nothing if it doesn't generate sales, traffic, customer leads, or other real business results. Worse, if it does any of that for your competitors instead, you deserve to be shown the door—pronto.

Most companies seem to understand that social media offers them an incredible opportunity to reach both new and existing customers they never could reach before, whether because of opportunity or cost, but few companies take the time to figure out what they really hope to get out of a word-of-mouth campaign. Office Max clearly had no idea what it wanted to generate with Elf Yourself. If we had to guess, we'd venture that the Elf Yourself idea just sounded too cool to pass up. After that, someone convinced Office Max that if it built Elf Yourself, consumers would come—and also buy. It's not that simple, though, as you surely know, having read this far. Ultimately, the campaign did virtually nothing to help traffic or sales. (Elf Yourself was a microsite—further proof that this brand of drive-by marketing just doesn't work.) Because Office Max failed to connect its brand to Elf Yourself, the company didn't get much of anything out of an otherwise incredibly successful campaign. It certainly got much, much less than it could have, and what's more, it lost a golden opportunity to become the leader, or at least number two, in a three-horse race.

Invariably, when we present the Elf Yourself case, people ask us what Office Max should've done. As you read this and likely other books on social-media marketing, take a moment to stop and ask yourself the same question. What would you have done in the face of some of the case studies? How would you make a questionable social-media campaign work using the principles of judo, and how could you make an already successful campaign perform even better for your company? Mull over these questions and consider them as a belt test of your social media judo expertise.

We identified a few key, easy-to-implement changes that could've improved Elf Yourself:

- Keep the content on your main site. Microsites (as we have discussed) are very tough to leverage for the core brand site and rarely forge strong ties with the main site, let alone the community and your customer base (this is in no small part because customers know that microsites have a finite expected lifespan).

- Focus on the benefits of the company and its products, not just engagement. Office Max didn't focus on its products, its benefits, or how it's different, so the Elf Yourself campaign amounted to little more than a memorable gimmick (although not when it came to the sponsoring brand). Compare this with Blendtec, which has focused its "Will it Blend?" program on the benefits of its blenders and designed its search-engine and keyword optimization to capitalize on the viral aspects of the campaign.

- Bring focus back to the stores. Office Max could've offered coupons for holiday gifts, customizable elf dolls for purchase, or free printouts of a customer's elf—anything that would get people into the store (be it the online or real-world iteration) for fulfillment and a chance for another sale or up-sell.

- Remember your demographics. Small businesses and office managers are the bulk of customers who frequent stores like Office Max, so why not make Elf Yourself an office holiday card that helped Office Max customers connect with their own customers? The campaign offered nothing targeted at small-business decision makers and purchasers; everything was geared as much for nontarget customers as for Office Max's core demographic.

Blendtec (willitblend.com) focused on the benefits of the product while highlighting the brand message (not just clever visuals for clever visuals' sake like Office Max's Elf Yourself).

Don't get us wrong, Elf Yourself wasn't a bad use of technology and social media. It would've been a lights-out winner for Coca-Cola, McDonalds, or another omnipresent, brand-centric company with broad appeal (plus, those companies would have leveraged this campaign to the hilt as we are suggesting), but Office Max spent far too much money on Elf Yourself and didn't focus enough of its effort on driving sales within its key target markets. The downloads, the site traffic, the links, and all the other details that make for a successful word-of-mouth campaign don't mean much if they don't somehow translate into sales or market-share gains at some point. It's not always a direct link to a sale, especially as companies incorporate social media across the entire span of the product cycle, but at some point, social media has to pay for itself, usually by improving sales. Otherwise, what's the point?

This is what a judo expert would call *ippon*. If the greatest test of judo skill is *shiai*, or open competition, the ultimate proof of a fighter's skill is the single point that seals the win. This is *ippon*. It's not just a point, it's *the* point. As Neil Ohlenkamp explains, a student's striving for that decisive point is fundamental to understanding all of judo. Now, let's be clear, judo isn't life or death—and neither is marketing through social media—but the goal of a contest is to approach it as if you don't get another chance and, in so doing, to seek perfection. A failed campaign or some negative buzz on the Web won't bankrupt your company (at least not all on its own), but there does in fact exist an *ippon* for companies doing word-of-mouth marketing through social media. The point of all this, as the point of all marketing efforts, is to get a return on your investment. As a company, you're not just marketing because you like to see your brand name floating around the Internet but to make more in revenues than you spend on marketing.

The whole goal of marketing through social media is to pay for itself and then some. If it doesn't, or doesn't have the potential to do so in time, you need to tweak your approach—or can it altogether. It should be low-cost, high-return across the board. That's the beauty of social media: You can get so much more from it than you pay for. Still, most companies shoot themselves in the foot from the start. They either shoot their left foot by spending a boatload on a campaign, which of course requires a huge increase in sales to generate a useful return, or shoot their right foot, treating social media as a disconnected add-on and depriving it of the planning necessary to ensure its success. Sometimes, they do both (witness Elf Yourself). Both approaches drive us nuts; with the possibility of returns vastly superior to most traditional marketing campaigns, why would a company shoot itself in either foot right from the start? A company need not set an unreachable bar or limit itself to mediocre returns, but finding the right level of investment and allocating the right resources to a campaign requires some work; planning a social media campaign cannot be a frivolous pursuit or done on a whim. A marketing department needs to know how social media supports other marketing efforts while also standing on its own. Marketers need to have a plan and put some rigor and process around their approach to online marketing. They need to identify their own *ippon*.

Stubbornness And Ignorance

If you've read this far and aren't convinced that you should pursue more word-of-mouth marketing campaigns, here's our one last shot at convincing you (and if you're already implementing your marketing through social media, here's some more evidence to prove your brilliance): Simply put, marketing professionals no longer can ignore the growing wave of evidence. The combination of social media, consumer-generated media, search results, and third-party endorsement from credible sources hits consumers precisely when and where consumers are making buying decisions. It's the ultimate swing at the sweet spot of customer decision-making.

When properly employed, social-media tools provide companies a more cost effective and potentially more powerful marketing program. The problem isn't convincing marketing professionals that social media can help their businesses but convincing those marketing professionals to do the extra legwork required to do social marketing the right way. This is where we repeatedly see marketers display a frustrating mix of laziness fueled by stubbornness or ignorance. The lazy, ignorant marketers use the quickest way to get credit for any kind of social-media success so they can claim they have hit their quarterly goals. The lazy, stubborn marketers are convinced they have it all figured out but don't have any real success to show for it. The stubborn side tends to be more dangerous for a business; the ignorant side is much more common. Ultimately, though, both sides end up making the same fundamental mistakes.

Many of our clients don't know what they want to accomplish when they come to us, and we end up playing the role of consultants in a far more basic sense. A lot of what we do involves asking the right questions to find out what the client wants, then steering the client in the right direction. We have to spell out the expectations and reorient the client in a direction that's going to pay dividends by building credibility for its brand, currying favor with influencers, or simply accomplishing whatever the client hopes to accomplish to move the business forward. That's not an easy thing to do, in large part because companies need to become active participants in the discussion occurring online. That's part of the fundamental philosophical shift we outlined earlier in this book, and that's not something that simply happens overnight.

Some straightforward steps should nevertheless be considered by every company when starting an online marketing campaign using social media. We ask these very questions of ourselves before setting out any plans with our clientele. Every campaign we see is different from the last, but none of them would work if we didn't first ask these questions and go through the same preparatory steps. The process starts with an analysis and audit of the current situation. Ask yourself:

- What's the state of the company's current marketing program, and how can social media augment our existing efforts?
- Where does the company want to go with its social-media marketing efforts? What does it want to accomplish with this campaign, and how does that position it to capitalize on the momentum created by the campaign?
- What are the business goals the company seeks to achieve, and how will success be measured against these goals?
- What's the appropriate influencer-engagement strategy to achieve those goals, and how does that break down into specific tactics for the company to most efficiently execute the plan?

Our guess is that this list is not much different from the questions you ask yourself before planning any good marketing campaign, but because few companies bother to look at social media as a part of their core marketing strategy, social media rarely gets the same degree of scrutiny that other campaigns would receive. Let's call a spade a spade— such activity is ignorance. Social media, judo marketing, word of mouth, or whatever you call it is sub-optimal as a duct-taped add-on to a broader marketing campaign. A company has to either craft a social-media campaign that has its own directive and its own goals, or make social media an integral part of an overall marketing campaign, measuring its performance in relation to the broader program. In today's environment, people are far too quick to praise campaigns that get customers to "do something" but that don't ever accomplish the ultimate goal of marketing: driving revenue growth, whether through direct sales, lead generation, reduced cost of acquisition, lower support costs, higher customer retention, or other means.

We see far too many marketers who focus on things they shouldn't, measuring things they shouldn't measure. You need not be that person! This isn't our chief concern, however, because the ignorance will evaporate as more marketing professionals learn what works and what doesn't stand up to executives' scrutiny. Instead, we worry about the marketing professionals who not only measure all the wrong things but also treat the results as sacred gospel. A stubborn, know-it-all approach immediately limits what a company can accomplish with such a low-cost, high-return medium.

We see companies that don't want to hear that they could accomplish so much more, and we struggle to convince them of something they have no interest in ever hearing. We can produce results for companies that focus on the wrong metrics; that's pretty easy. It's much harder to get such companies to consider the other possibilities that they insist on glossing over or missing entirely. We had clients who couldn't track more than 80% of their inbound leads from online sources using

Omniture. They focused on the smaller 20% of "trackable" leads and tried optimizing within that group, refusing to adopt new processes that could optimize the other 80% of the leads that went largely unidentified (not to mention their avoidance of fixing their tracking system). In that environment, the small number of leads they could track got a disproportionately large share of the budget, even though Google searches and other leads without specifically assigned reference codes still generated a much greater share of their sales and traffic. Until these companies fix the larger problem, banner ads will seem like their greatest marketing vehicle, while all the others marketing will then be seen as "less successful than banner ads."

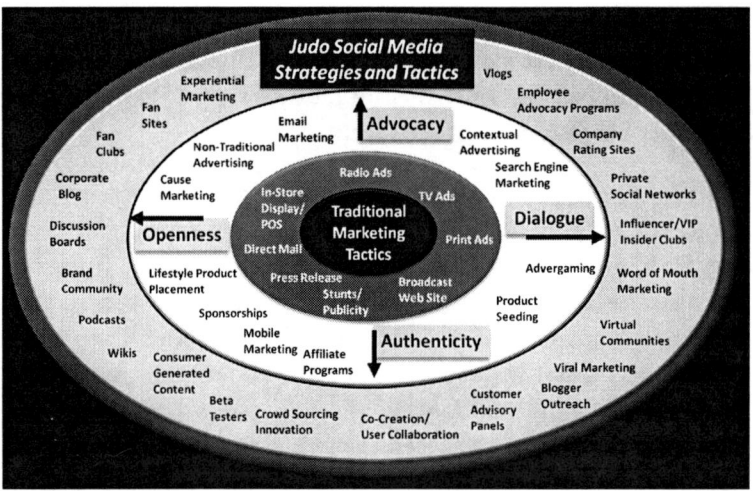

In creating Judo social-media campaigns, marketers have a wealth of tactics at their disposal (a small sample is represented in the outer ring), and influencers can and will help drive efforts across the board.

We've put on some remarkably successful campaigns in an effort to increase search rankings and online "share of voice," but these companies could have done far more. We see companies who congratulate themselves for a brilliant single slice of a word-of-mouth marketing program while the rest of the marketing pie rots away and amounts to very little. Companies have a golden opportunity to back-foot the competition and put their rivals in a completely reactive mode, but instead, they choose to focus on a limited set of strategies—and on the limited return brought about by them. Whether they do this out of ignorance or stubbornness doesn't really matter. Whatever is driving this behavior, the opportunities remain available for everyone—including the competition—to capitalize on.

All The Possibilities

We led off this book with a story about the Windows Vista launch because it so wonderfully illustrates the importance of learning as much from success as from failure. We can't stress enough how important that is, and here's why: The only way to make sure you aren't limiting your projects, measuring the wrong results, or leaving opportunities for your rivals is to openly critique and evaluate everything you do. Marketing professionals have to become naturally suspicious of the word-of-mouth campaigns that work. The evolving social-media atmosphere is changing too rapidly and offers too many new tools, platforms, and possibilities to leave the successes unexamined. Seen another way, there's no case to be made for starting with self-congratulations for today's success when leading off tomorrow's program.

Some of the clients we mentioned in this chapter celebrate how well they capitalize on the 20% of leads they can track. (This is more than one client, but is it also you?) Rather than seeking ways to increase that fraction, they simply look for ways to optimize that 20%. A lot of campaigns *feel* successful, and success is addictive, of course: "Look at us, we made something happen!" At Ivy Worldwide, we don't suggest that marketers should stop enjoying that drug—heck, it's some good stuff—we just hope that more companies and marketing professionals realize there are better pharmaceuticals available—in other words, drugs that cost less, do more, and cure exactly what ails your company. Marketing groups need to put in the work to find those drugs and figure out how to use them; there are no shortcuts in that regard. We've met far too many marketing professionals strung out on all kinds of useless social-media drugs. Some mainline traffic numbers, fans, followers, or other nonsense. Others get their fix from little bumps in search-engine rankings. The campaigns look good, the success feels great, but the real impact is immeasurable and the full potential far from realized. Elf Yourself is a classic example, but Office Max isn't alone in this equation.

Chick-fil-A has done a decent job of engaging some key influencers, including one who started a Facebook page for the fast-food joint. The company now feeds the page's administrator everything from store-opening information to promotions, and the page now has more than 1 million followers. Chick-fil-A even uses its Facebook page to generate feedback on new ideas. For the most part, it has used the site thoughtfully, but one particular promotion struck us as odd and largely useless, and it's emblematic of a company not having a full grasp of social media. Around Labor Day one year, the company used Facebook as part of a marketing campaign that offered 250,000 people coupons for a free chicken sandwich. By the end of it, Chick-fil-A could say it had thousands of people who'd signed up on its Facebook page, but it really hadn't engaged them in any meaningful way, or in a way that lent itself to consistency. It had succeeded in spawning no real word of mouth for itself other than getting people to sign up for a free sandwich, and one that probably ended up costing more than was recouped via increased sales.

At its core, the Chick-fil-A campaign was immeasurable on the metrics that, in the end, really matter. The company could boast of large engagement volumes and all its new Facebook friends, but how many of the people who'd friended them did so simply for the free sandwich and never bothered to go back to the page for anything else? Like so many campaigns, this particular piece of Chick-fil-A's approach wasn't designed to be measured in any meaningful, long-term sense. We have no problem with programs designed to generate buzz and interest in the short term, but those programs don't mean anything if they don't also spawn more sales, a heightened sense of brand loyalty, or some meaningful marketing goal. To capitalize on the full potential of online marketing, marketing professionals have to start thinking in terms of generating value that's both tangible and measurable over the long haul.

Remember that word-of-mouth and social media is an ongoing process; it is not anywhere near a fire-and-forget type of marketing activity. The goal of any type of campaign or program is to get long-term evangelism and endorsement from truly influential individuals. Our value to our clients and your value to your organization is the ability to repeat the success over and over again. This is not to say that companies shouldn't be measuring the core metrics of individual campaigns. Every campaign should include an evaluation of the volume (the number of people talking), the sentiment (the tone of what they're saying), and the topics (the brand-related issues about which they're talking). Those are core metrics. But every campaign also should consider more advanced issues, such as those below.

- Reach: How broad is the audience that's viewing consumer-generated media about your brand, and how are you engaging that audience?
- Dispersion: The number and types of communities where the buzz is happening, including sites whose owners you're not directly engaging, and also any propagation into mainstream media outlets
- Influence: The ability of an influencer, blogger, or online participant to create buzz, usually quantified by some sort of measure of commentary as well as propensity for propagation via other parties
- Emotion: The percentage of community messages that matches a particular sentiment about the brand
- Impact: The connection of the buzz to sales or other predetermined goals

- Permanence: The length of time a topic remains under active discussion within your customer base

These are the second and third layers of activity measurement that demonstrate the creation of real connections between a company and its customers, and also between marketing campaigns and every marketer's ultimate goal: to foster greater sales growth. Most companies get stuck at the surface layers, focusing on the flashy core metrics like 1 million Facebook friends or raw site traffic. Few businesses have really pushed themselves to plumb the deeper strata, to find out whether their flash-in-the-pan marketing campaigns have left any lasting impressions on their communities of customers—and, if they did, what those impressions are and how the companies can use the impressions to affect their bottom-line results.

The ultimate value of any social media campaign has to be measured by these second-level measures, not just those of the first-level, and as with any objective in a marketing campaign, marketing departments and managers have to research and define these goals in advance of launching into a new program. Far too many marketers are happy to walk away from a campaign with some of that first-level data, adding it into their performance reviews and leaving all the rest to wither away. They abandon the word-of-mouth marketing campaign's real and greater value through lack of full understanding of what it can accomplish. They give up the chance to create a lasting impression, one that generates true brand loyalty and enjoys long-term influence on purchasing decisions.

Even fewer companies have tapped the full potential of social media beyond promotions and product launches. As we explained in Chapter 4, social media can benefit the entire product cycle if it's fully implemented. This again comes with proper planning and design, and it can indeed be measured. A company can track how much useful product-design feedback it gets from the online community, and it can use that information to adjust the program so as to glean even better and more relevant ideas for future product iterations. The marketing department can tap into the same community expertise to guide its product launch and other campaigns, striking the right balance of online and offline efforts to spur the most sales in the process. Sometimes social media provides ways to conduct market research or troubleshoot and support a product issue in ways that are significantly cheaper than traditional techniques. Most companies leave far too much on the table when they take too narrow a view of their social-media marketing, and that won't change until the evaluation of the program digs deeper than the surface-level successes.

Leaving A Lasting Impression

Every social media campaign has a half-life. Most campaigns go by like a blip on a screen and are never heard of again. A handful will glow for years. As you would expect, a campaign done in a piecemeal fashion will fade faster than a marketing department can replace it. A thoughtful, well-planned, and multilayered program can hang around the top end of search-engine rankings and influence purchasing inclinations for months, even years. All of this is predicated on the depth of involvement and relationship with your industry's influencers, the latter of which should last a lifetime.

Life changes rapidly in the social media environment, and it's easy to see the goal as one of hit-and-run, get in and get out. There is no doubt that the company that plods about the blogosphere will be left in the dust, but customers don't act on the same timetable that runs the social media world; they purchase on their own time, so a company's online program does little good if it fades quickly and misses the ongoing interest of current and potential customers. A properly designed, executed, and evaluated social media campaign will have a half-life long enough to renew itself, either by the company or its customers, successfully engaging customers on their own terms.

The notion of permanence doesn't necessarily come easily in the online world, where standards of measure are still evolving and it seems everything is in constant upheaval, but it can (and should) happen, and social media provides the best opportunity to create a lasting impression. The company that builds relationships with influencers, designs and measures its programs on a richer set of criteria, and looks to give back as much to the community as it gets from its efforts will start to see its messages linger and its allies stand beside it longer. It will enjoy a dynamic authority, and its customers will take heed of the third-party endorsements as they research upcoming purchases. On those occasions when the company does screw up—and everyone screws up at one time or another—it will have a long and public track record to help cushion any fall.

Every now and then, a company will do its homework and put together a campaign that's ready-made to succeed. It'll hit at just the right time with just the right message, and it will deliver the full potential of marketing through social media. It doesn't come easy, and it doesn't come all the time, but when it does, it glows forever.

CONCLUSION

Time To Get Out There And Do It

NOT LONG AFTER WE REALIZED we had to write a book, we started discussing all the logistics we'd have to tackle along the way. We pondered whether we should self-publish or pitch the manuscript to a professional publishing house. We tossed around different ideas for the right release date. We debated different people who might write a foreword for us. Being novice authors, the whole process was entirely new to us.

The one piece we never worried about was how we'd spread the word about the book. We knew the judo philosophy of social media was not only the topic but one of the key ways to sell this book. We know of no better way to market a product—whether a book, a notebook, or an e-book reader—than word-of-mouth or social-media judo. We pored through our database of blogger and content-producer friends to help write this book, so we naturally turned to them when it came time to sell it, too. Unless you're related to us, chances are pretty good that at least half of you found out about this book from one of the many influencers with whom we work. That's not coincidence—it's the whole point. If we didn't have supreme confidence in our approach, you wouldn't be reading this book today.

This is just the starting point, however. One doesn't become an expert at social-media marketing simply by reading this book, any more than one becomes a judo master simply by reading a set of instructions. You have to get out there and practice the craft. No one will argue with the fact that it's easier said than done, but a company looking to get the biggest marketing bang for the smallest buck has to learn how to tap into the reach and momentum that online communities offer. And there's no way to do that without —you guessed it—simply going out and doing it. So, in hopes of easing the way, we'll leave you with a few parting bits of advice.

Start With An Open Mind

It might sound odd to read it here at the end of the book, but no one can tell you precisely how online marketing works. In fact, run away from anyone who suggests he or she can. If you've made it this far and think we've given you a foolproof blueprint for your next word-of-mouth campaign, we've failed and you'll find yourself in the same position as our friends at Toshiba and DuPont—running programs that look a lot like 31 Days of the Dragon but achieving none of the same success. We have no secret sauce, no key for unlocking the secrets of online communities and how they react to marketing messages. What we do have is the proper mindset, the proper judo philosophy for approaching an online community, and although that doesn't guarantee success, the refusal to shift one's mindset to accommodate the fundamentally social and interactive nature of online communities will guarantee failure.

So, start with an open mind. Marketing professionals who reach out to key online influencers with inquiring minds, asking instead of telling, will find a whole new set of experts ready and willing to help. They'll realize that the governors of these online communities have invaluable customer insights that they're willing and eager to share. They'll realize that those same influencers will vouch for them when honest mistakes happen. They'll find that they have a whole new set of *expert* voices who can offer product-development advice based on the preferences expressed by millions of potential and existing customers. Simply put, the age of the top-down, know-it-all corporate marketing department is over. Customers now have a wealth of forums to announce what they like and what they don't like. The company that learns to listen to its customers—not just hear them, but actually *listen* to them—will win in today's hypermediated marketplace.

Throw out the idea that you know your customers better than anyone else possibly could. Even if it's true—and that's a massive "if" these days—there's still much to learn from others, especially your company's key influencers, who interact with those customers every day. Go to these influencers with an open mind, willing to help them succeed, and they'll help you do the same. They'll open up a new world of insight into your customer base.

Make Some New Friends

There's a reason some insightful character coined the term "social media." The fundamental success of everything from blogs to Facebook to Twitter stems from the user's ability to interact with other users—their ability to be social creatures. Sociologists point to real-life, interpersonal interaction as the basis for both local and global communities—and, to a great extent, humankind's continued existence as a species—so why, in a virtual world created by these selfsame humans, would we expect to find anything different? Lest we get too academic here, we'll ask the question more bluntly: People want to interact with other people, so why has interacting with other people become so anathema to corporations?

At some point, every marketer has to participate in a true interaction with some of his or her customers. Why so few marketing professionals seek to do that as often as possible is beyond us. We might've bought that excuse 10 years ago, when making those direct, interpersonal connections required a lot of effort, resources, money, and time, but with the rise of social media, those old excuses go out the window. Yes, the invaluable face-to-face meetings still require a lot of money, time, and effort, but social media provide a new, inexpensive, and easy platform for effective virtual interactions to maintain the

Is this the future of online marketing, or are you kidding yourself into thinking this is the only way to use social media to sell products? (From: http://wheresmyjetpack.blogspot.com.)

connection between face-to-face episodes. Don't be afraid to interact as a consequence, as greater interaction is where it's all headed, anyway. Consider those customers willing to make virtual connections as potential friends. In a phrase, be social.

Let us clarify, though, that no one person, or even marketing department, has enough time on his or her hands to monitor every Web site and respond to every customer request. That's the very reason the judo philosophy is such an invaluable metaphor to working on social media. By befriending and working in a mutually beneficial manner with key online influencers, a company can leverage its influencers' credibility, insight, and broad reach. An influencer who feels like he or she has the ear of a company will be happy to work with that company. Despite the popular perception, the blogosphere is not full of people who want only to bash every product they see and expose the smallest of flaws. In fact, when it comes to a company's key influencers, the truth is

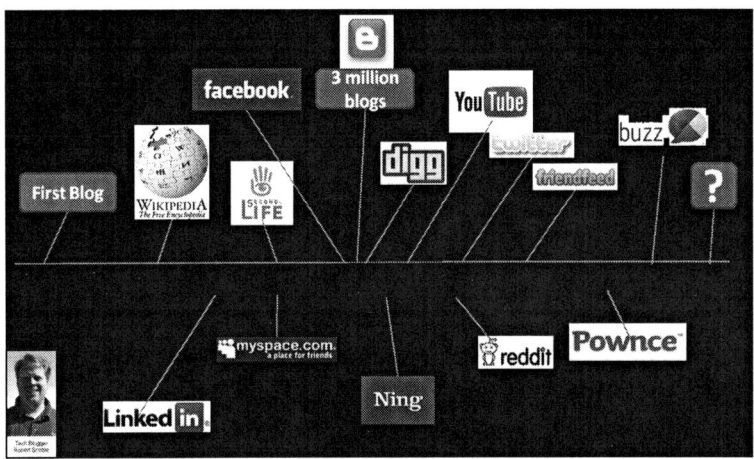

As social media technologies and platforms change and evolve over time, marketers are tempted to jump on each one new platform or portal. Yet, there is one thing that is constant – the influencers as this a medium driven by the people. Robert Scoble, like all influencers, has been on all of these platforms and many more and asked his readers to follow him every step of the way. If we want to contact him, however, we just call him. In an age of new technology every second, the telephone and face-to-face meetings are still far more effective to building credibility and evangelists.

quite the opposite; they want you to offer a good product that addresses their wants and needs. Befriend them, and they'll be happy to help you develop, and then sell, that very product.

Don't Be Bashful

A friend once gave us some ingenious advice for a visit to Cairo. His suggestion: Just accept the fact that you're going to get ripped off. From taxi drivers to merchants in the nearby souk, the locals would end up charging us far more than any straight-thinking Egyptian would pay. Accept it as part of a visit to a developing country, our friend suggested, and realize that the difference was essentially peanuts once we factored in the currency conversion rates and our first-world standard of living. Even with his advice, it took a day or two to truly come to terms with the eerie feeling that we were paying far too much, but once we came to terms with it, we found ourselves freed of many concerns and were able to truly enjoy our day-to-day experience in that remarkable and fascinating country.

We're not about to suggest that companies accept getting ripped off in the virtual world, nor would we suggest they tacitly accept all the criticism that inevitably will come their way, but there's no disputing the fact that companies go into the online ecosystem as strangers in a strange land—their collective actions demonstrate as much. The companies that look only to conservatively protect themselves at every turn will garner all the more criticism and ill will from the natives. Companies that reach out, forge relationships, take chances to try new things, and acknowledge the inevitable slip-ups with grace and confidence will earn the respect and support of the blogosphere.

Charlene Li, one of the most popular social-media experts, suggests that companies with a perfect track record simply aren't trying hard enough. Fortune favors the bold—the old cliché holds true in the blogosphere as well as and perhaps more so than in the real world. Companies that aren't bashful and that dare to try interesting new things can accomplish some remarkable feats online. Given the volatile nature of the blogosphere, the ever-changing social-media tools, and the constantly morphing desires of the billions of consumers who research, window-shop, and buy online, however, companies are bound to make mistakes from time to time. The companies that go in with open minds, build real relationships with influencers, and add value for the community will succeed despite the occasional mistake.

Don't Worry, People Not As Smart As You Are Succeeding

For the marketing folks who have made the leap and tried working through social media, pretty much all of this will sound like common sense. The dirty little secret is that this whole thing *is* common sense. We have no corner on the market for social media or word-of-mouth expertise. What we've done is strike out with the very mindset necessary to generate truly successful word-of-mouth marketing campaigns over and over again for differing clients in differing markets.

We fretted a bit when we started writing this book, worried that we'd somehow tip our hand and show anyone and everyone how to match our success, but we soon realized that our approach wasn't one born of ingenious insight or some sparkling revelation. Our success is rooted in our ability to believe fully in the social, open-minded, and mutually beneficial approach that a judo philosophy dictates. Our success doesn't grow from some incredible gimmick that we can patent and no one else can match but from an utterly basic willingness to accept a common-sense approach that benefits us, our clients, and the key online influencers with whom we work.

The irony is that this is the hardest piece for companies to adopt. We have no remarkable twist on the judo mindset and philosophy; we've just come to a comprehensive realization that giving ourselves over to it results in the greatest success. So many people coming from traditional marketing don't want to give themselves over to that same realization without some kind of artificial blueprint or plan—and that's the advantage for those of us who can manage to actually give in and adopt the necessary mindset.

We do this well because, once you do it, it's remarkably easy to continue doing well. So go out and try, fail, succeed, and learn. Be open to criticism and guidance in your approach, and at the end of the day, you'll learn—as the judo student does— that success becomes much easier when you tap into the all the momentum available to you.